D0780242

LOST CLASSICS

Lost Classics

EDITED BY

Michael Ondaatje

Michael Redhill

Esta Spalding

Linda Spalding

ALFRED A. KNOPF CANADA

Published by
Alfred A. Knopf Canada

 Published in 2000 by Alfred A. Knopf Canada, a division of Random House of Canada Limited, Toronto. Distributed by Random House of Canada Limited, Toronto.

Essays by the following contributors were originally published, some in a slightly different form, in *Brick: A Literary Journal*, numbers 61-63: Margaret Atwood, Murray Bail, Russell Banks, Anne Carson, George Elliott Clarke, Robert Creeley, Douglas Fetherling, Charles Foran, Helen Garner, Michael Helm, Greg Hollingshead, Isabel Huggan, Laird Hunt, John Irving, Pico Iyer, Janice Kulyk Keefer, Alan Lightman, David Malouf, Harry Mathews, Erin Mouré, Michael Redhill, Joanna Scott, Sarah Sheard, Esta Spalding, Sharon Thesen, Colm Toibin, Edmund White.

Design: CS Richardson

Canadian Cataloguing in Publication Data

Lost classics

ISBN 0-676-97299-3

1. Literature—History and criticism.
2. Authors—Books and reading.
I. Ondaatje, Michael, 1943– .

PN45.L65 2000 809 C00-931397-4

First Edition

Printed and bound in the United States of America

10 9 8 7 6 5 4 3 2 1

Page XI illustration: "About Camping They Were Never Wrong, the Old Masters" (detail), adapted from J. Adams' "The Surprise Visit," 1942. From *Brick*, number 61, winter 1998.
Page 9 photograph: courtesy of the Estate of Elisabeth Dennys. *Pages 204 and 205 photographs:* from *Othello*, Castle Rock Productions, Inc.

CONTENTS

INTRODUCTION

A BOOK THAT WE LOVE haunts us forever; it will haunt us, even when we can no longer find it on the shelf or beside the bed where we must have left it. After all, it is the act of reading, for many of us, that forged our first link to the world. And so lost books—books that have gone missing through neglect or been forgotten in changing tastes or worst of all, gone up in a puff of rumour—gnaw at us. Being lovers of books, we've pulled a scent of these absences behind us our whole reading lives, telling people about books that exist only on our own shelves, or even just in our own memory. This is what was on our minds one rainy afternoon in Toronto, as we sat around a dining-room table where the four of us, every few months, make manifest a sporadic but long-lived magazine called *Brick: A Literary Journal*.

By 1998, when we conceived of the "Lost Classics" issue, *Brick* had become a neighbourhood, full of essays and interviews that in turn became an international conversation: writers caught weeding, caught chatting over fences, full of chagrin and sometimes surprised to recognize each other after a season's quiet. So it felt natural to begin by asking some of our long-time contributors to tell us the story of a book loved and lost, books that had been overlooked or under-read, that had been stolen and never retrieved, or that were long out of print. We wanted personal stories and they began to pour in.

"Back in 1983, the novel received a fair amount of well-deserved attention …" John Irving wrote of *The Headmaster's Papers*, with a note of premonitory despair. Margaret Atwood described a Swedish novel, a tattered paperback found in a second-hand bookstore. "On the back of my copy are various encomiums, from the *Observer*, the *Guardian*, the *Sunday Telegraph*, the *Glasgow Herald*—'a masterpiece,' 'the most remarkable book of the year,' and so forth. Still, as far as I know, *Doctor Glas* has long been out of print, at least in its English version."

Helen Garner recalled meeting the author of a beloved childhood book, unknown by anyone she knew but that she remembered vividly. "A real Australian person had written it!" she noted triumphantly. "We corresponded. I asked if she had a spare copy. She said she had only one left, but would lend it to me if I promised to return it. In due course it arrived. I hardly dared to open it. But when I did, out of its battered pages flowed in streams, uncorrupted, the same scary joy it had brought me as a child, before everything in my life had happened."

Before everything had happened. Before even the beloved book was entirely lost. The "Lost Classics" issue, as we called it, struck a chord that kept sounding long after publication. Essays continued to pour in on longed-for books of poetry, children's stories, travel diaries, novels. Why not a *book* of lost classics? More stories. More lost love.

Some of the newer essays describe a child's love affair with literature that is the beginning of a writerly discipline. The young reader discovers a place to enter another world and uses it as escape. Or, refuses to come out. As Robert Creeley says, "When young, I longed for someone who would talk to me and, often as not, that person was found in a book." If childhood stories are where we learn about plot, rhythm and narrative, they also teach us morals, while explaining the darker side of human nature. We read them when we are most susceptible and over the years they continue to inhabit and sustain us.

The essays we have selected for this collection are such memories of reading: they are that dialogue with the mind of an absent other, that conversation both silent and shared, that moment when a reader seems to have found the perfect mate. But loving is a unique torment if the beloved isn't known to friends, family, the unwilling listener who must be convinced. Many versions of lostness are investigated here. There is the book that disappears from the house during a divorce, and a lost manuscript that becomes a cult classic. There is the writer who commits suicide after finishing his work, and a reader who exhumes it from the remainder bin. There are the missing libraries of India and a book that survived in spite of the odds. The essays we've chosen come from all over the world and the books are of every kind. But lost books are like dying languages: the fewer the people who remember them, the greater the risk that they will disappear for good. When, for whatever reason, a book that means much is lost, there is the need to write a eulogy, an explanation, a defence.

Perhaps this anthology maps the inner lives of its contributors. Perhaps we are set in our ways through the books that we've loved. The book mentioned to a young Harry Mathews at a grown-up cocktail party, for example, infected his imagination so seriously, that many years later, he tracked it down. And stole it. The primer called *I Want to Go to School*, published by the People's Publishing House of China, set Anchee Min in the direction of her writing life. One book enumerates a system of imaginary knowledge. Another causes a journey. There are lost survival manuals and lost warnings.

Like the magazine itself, our anthology is a conversation. Michael Helm remembers a book of poetry by Philip Levine, while Levine remembers another book of poetry. Eden Robinson writes about awakening to science fiction as a teenager in Kitamaat Village. Others write of Shangri-La and Islandia. Rudy Wiebe describes the strange foretelling of his sister's death. Russell Banks discovers a lost companion to Graham Greene's *Journey Without Maps*, and Cassandra Pybus writes of a lost partner to Elizabeth Smart's *By Grand Central Station I Sat Down and Wept*. Caryl Phillips conjures Orson Welles; W. S. Merwin digs up an archeological classic; and Nancy Huston recalls a knell unheard. And, reminding us of the whole enterprise of writing in the first place, Laird Hunt quotes Borges on "a certain class of objects, very rare, that are brought into being by hope." A perfect description of this anthology about books we have loved and lost and loved again.

—The Editors, *Brick: A Literary Journal*

MARGARET ATWOOD

❋

Doctor Glas—Hjalmar Söderberg

> Now I sit at my open window, writing—for whom? Not for any friend or mistress. Scarcely for myself, even. I do not read today what I wrote yesterday; nor shall I read this tomorrow. I write simply so my hand can move, my thoughts move of their own accord. I write to kill a sleepless hour. Why can't I sleep? After all, I've committed no crime.

THIS SHORT, ASTONISHING NOVEL arrived in the mail a couple of years ago, sent by Swedish friends who ferret in second-hand bookstores in search of Swedish books in translation which they think I might like. They were spot-on with this one.

Doctor Glas was first published in 1905 and caused a scandal then, in Sweden, for reasons that had to do with its handling of those two scandalous items, sex and death—not to mention their sub-sets, abortion and euthanasia. The version I have is a tattered paperback from 1970, a reissue of a 1963 translation—published I suppose to coincide with a film based on it, directed incidentally by Mai Zetterling. On the back of my copy are various encomiums, from the *Observer*, the *Guardian*, the *Sunday Telegraph*, the *Glasgow Herald*—"a masterpiece," "the most remarkable book of the year," and so forth. Still, as far as I know, *Doctor Glas* has long been out of print, at least in its English version.

The narrator of *Doctor Glas* is Doctor Glas, a thirtyish man whose journal we *hypocrites lecteurs* read over his shoulder as he composes it. His is the remarkable yet unnervingly familiar voice we follow in its reflections, its prevarications, its self-denunciations, its boredoms, its wistfulness, its lyrical praises or splenetic denunciations of the weather. A romantic idealist turned solitary and sad, afflicted with fin-de-siècle malaise, pestered by thoughts of Darwin and duty, Baudelaire and escapism, the longing for love and action, and the sceptical inertia of his age,

The Atlantic Monthly Press edition © 1963

unable to fall in love except with women who are in love with someone else, infested by his own unconscious—of which he is fitfully conscious—he offers both the candid transparency and the narcissism his surname would suggest.

However, it's no accident that his second name is Gabriel, for he is tempted to play Angel of Life to a beautiful woman who arrives at his surgery one day begging for his help. Ignorant of what marriage entails, she has allowed herself to be pawned off on a "respectable" but morally and physically loathsome clergyman. The help she wants from Glas is freedom from this troll's sexual attentions, which she finds repugnant in the extreme—especially since she is having an affair with another man. Doctor Glas takes pity on her and invents a disease for her, and lies to the husband about it for her sake. Thus it begins. Angels can of course be angels of death as well as of life, and doctors are very conveniently situated for this role. I won't spoil the plot by telling what happens next, but it's a cunning triple-tied knot.

Doctor Glas is deeply unsettling, in the way certain dreams are—or, no coincidence, certain films by Bergman, who must have read it. It moves from the sordid to the banal to the anxiously surreal to the visionary with economy and impressive style. A few years earlier and it would never have been published; a few years later and it would have been dubbed a forerunner of stream-of-consciousness. It occurs on the cusp of our century, opening doors we've been opening ever since.

> And now, as I sit at my open window, writing this by a flickering candle—I detest touching oil lamps and my housekeeper is sleeping too soundly after her funeral coffee and cakes for me to have the heart to wake her—now, as the candleflame flutters in the draught and my shadow shivers and flutters like the flame on the wallpaper, as if trying to come to life—now I think of Hans Andersen and his tale of the shadow. And it seems to me I am the shadow who wished to become a man.

Murray Bail

The Fish Can Sing—Halldor Laxness
Frost—Thomas Bernhard
The Private Diaries of Stendhal—Stendhal

ANY NOVEL WHICH HAS as its first sentence "A wise man once said that next to losing its mother, there is nothing more healthy for a child than to lose its father" immediately stamps the author as one above the ordinary. From those words, enough to make all good people blink, or at least sit up and think, Halldor Laxness's *The Fish Can Sing* (Methuen, 1966) grows, and turns deeper and deeper, leading the reader into a new, entirely convincing world—a small world, mostly on the outskirts of Reykjavik, as if that matters, where memorable events unfold, concentrating on a small group of indelible characters. It is a novel (a world) that transmits something of the wonder of life, its strangeness, its goodness, occasions for stubbornness, and the stoicism of people—of people everywhere—at times very funny, which further deepens the "human-ness." It is written in a calm manner, to just the right length. *The Fish Can Sing* has been out of print for about thirty years. Perhaps the title is the trouble—a publisher's stumbling block? Is there a slightly frosty condescension towards anything written in a place as small and sparse as Iceland, better known for producing cod? Inevitably though, such a work of wonder will, as this small recommendation shows, attract readers, and give this work of art its "second life."

I would like to see Thomas Bernhard's 1965 first novel, *Frost,* translated and placed on the shelves of bookstores everywhere. Of course I haven't actually read it—it's in German—but by now it must be plain to even the most casual page-turner that anything by Bernhard is worth reading. There will always be something there. He is fearless, far from trivial, very strong and urgent in what he says. Although Bernhard writes in the first person, his novels are mercifully not self-confessional, let alone melodramatic or breathless, and that's refreshing enough. He also is appallingly funny. The one weakness is that after putting down a Thomas Bernhard book most other novels seem feeble and unnecessary. It would be interesting to see in his first work, *Frost*, how it all began.

If this survey is confined to the twentieth century, Stendhal does not qualify; yet his self-obsession (although he was extremely wary of the first person "I") is peculiarly modern. Besides, it is a scandal that *The Private Diaries of Stendhal* (Gollanz) has been out of print for verging on fifty years; to my knowledge there has never even been a paperback. As always the reader is quickly involved in Stendhal's happiness, or rather, his quest for it. In part, this explains the marvellous intimacy of style, a tossed-off quality, as though he is confiding, not really composing, a book. And it is as if we, readers, are actually looking over his shoulder.

The diaries begin:

> "I'm undertaking to write the history of my life day by day. I don't know whether I'll have the fortitude to carry out this plan, which I already started in Paris. There's a mistake in French already; there will be a lot more, because I'm making it a rule not to stand on ceremony and never to erase..."

He is forever scrutinizing his emotions. Much of his diary is spent analyzing his progress in seducing such and such a woman in society, usually where he went wrong. And there is an amazing scene in Moscow, with Napoleon, looking on as the old city is torched by the retreating Russians, and Stendhal interrupting his description to record a toothache.

Russell Banks

Too Late to Turn Back—Barbara Greene

In 1936, Barbara Greene, a twenty-two-year-old, slightly ditzy, naive, and utterly charming Londoner, a socialite some eight or nine years younger than her dour, somewhat secretive, literary cousin, Graham, agreed to join Greene on a walk from Sierra Leone across the vast uncharted jungle of Liberia. While drinking champagne together at a London party, Greene had confessed that he could find no one to join him. "I agreed at once. It sounded fun. Liberia, wherever it was, had a jaunty sound about it. Liberia! The more I said it to myself the more I liked it." She never says why Greene was making this months-long walk through a trackless equatorial jungle, nor does he, but we can guess that he was on a British espionage mission to observe the movements of Germany's colonial and military operations in West Africa. They brought plenty of quinine and several cases of Scotch and many cartons of tinned meat which they came to loathe. For her, it began as a lark, but soon it was too late to turn back—thus the title. She kept a journal and made herself into a shrewd, careful, compassionate observer of both her cousin the writer and Liberia. When she returned to London, a much wiser woman than before, she wrote her modest book, which is an intimate, brilliant portrait of Graham Greene as a young, angst-ridden, Catholic adventurer. Not incidentally, it is also a first-hand, first-rate description of a people and place that had not been described in detail before by any European. She turned out to be surprisingly tough, both physically and mentally, and the trek turned out to be nightmarish and cruel. She also happened to become, in the process, a fine writer of English prose, although I don't believe she ever wrote another book. Graham Greene

Barbara and Graham Greene in Liberia

wrote his own version of the trek, *Journey Without Maps*, in which he mentions his cousin by name only once and, as Paul Theroux points out in his introduction to *Too Late to Turn Back*, refers to her in passing as "my cousin" barely eleven times in three hundred pages. His book is still very much in print (Penguin). As far as I know, Barbara Greene's much better book was last published (with Theroux's fine introduction) in 1981 by Settle and Bendall (UK) and is now out of print. The great pleasure is to read them in tandem, his first, then hers.

Christian Bök

Codex Seraphinianus—Luigi Serafini

The *Codex Seraphinianus* by Luigi Serafini is an other-worldly encyclopedia—an incunabulum, bequeathed to us by some monk from a fantastic monastery in an alternate dimension.

Steve McCaffery, the avant-garde poet, introduced me to this marvellous catalogue years ago during one of my visits to his private library. This book enthralled me more than any of the other illuminated manuscripts in his collection. The cover of the black folio depicted a mattress, upon which two lovers, embracing, fused slowly together, until they formed a crocodile, crawling off the bed. I opened the book to discover a florilegium of pastel images, all of them captioned by an alien genre of cursive writing—meticulous arabesques, vaguely reminiscent of Sinhalese alphabets. I saw numerous diagrams depicting a variety of surreal objects in cartoonish landscapes: eyeball eggshells hatching into eyeglasses; serpent shoelaces latching onto ankleflesh—even an automobile melting into a white sticky gum, covered with houseflies. I had never before seen such a wilfully quixotic picture-book—and I spent hours thereafter, poring over the colourful menagerie of mutant animals and hybrid devices.

The *Codex* is a work of natural history, more bizarre than any treatise by Linnaeus or Alembert, since the *Codex* functions as a pataphysical extravagance, describing an arcane system of imaginary knowledge (not unlike a genre of science fiction, which shows science itself to be a fiction). The *Codex* summarizes the secret wisdom of a mythic empire: its alchemy, its zoology, its physics, its poetics. The book depicts an eerie world of oneiric madness: yarnballs walking on two legs through sunny gardens; umbrellas walking on two legs through rainy streets. A pedestrian, seemingly acephalic, steps onto a leopardskin rug, only to explode into the form of a jaguar. A man, whose head is a weathervane, turns his gaze to follow a leaf blown away upon an autumn breeze. A skywriting helicopter spray-paints the clouds with a knotted rainbow. A crystal galleon sails upon a tradewind generated by its own bellows. A reader of such a lavish volume quickly embarks upon a tour of exotic wonders and poetic marvels.

The *Codex* calls to mind the enigma of the Voynich Manuscript—a treatise attributed to the medieval sorcerer Roger Bacon, who appears to have drawn pictures not only of unknown flora and bizarre fauna, but of amoebic bacilli and stellar nebulae—phenomena depicted by him long before the invention of magnifiers and telescopes (and to this day, not even the most renowned cryptographers with the most advanced supercomputers have deciphered this ciphertext). Like the Voynich Manuscript, the *Codex* invites cryptanalysis. The signs used in the nonsensical calligraphy do demonstrate a statistical recurrence, whose patterns evoke a sense of grammatical rationalism. The book provides an image of a Rosetta Stone that might aid in translation, yet the accompanying, hieroglyphic text is itself untranslatable. The book implies that language itself acts as a wanton entity, its graffiti engraved everywhere throughout a protean reality (be it in the twists of a root or in the cracks of a wall)—and under magnification, the cursive writing on the page reveals itself to be a current full of fish or a highway full of cars. The letters of the text float away on little dirigibles or float down on little parachutes.

Douglas R. Hofstadter (in his *Metamagical Themas*) has remarked that the unearthliness of this book instills unease, if not terror, in many of his friends who peruse it, since the book appears to suggest that our quotidian existence may dissolve at any moment into something monstrous.

The *Codex* calls to mind the story by Borges about the fictional cosmology of Tlön—an unreal domain that steadily replaces the actual cosmos, as more and more people, reading about the universe of Tlön, forfeit their memories of the Real: "Already a fictitious past occupies in our memories the place of another, a past of which we know nothing with certainty—not even that it is false." The *Codex* aspires to convince us that its psychedelic dreamscapes are far more substantive than our own environment, and I often feel, when I flip through this book, that I risk looking up to find myself teleported to the twilight zone of Dementia Five—unable to return.

I have looked everywhere for a copy of this rare book, but I have never found it in stock at any of the antiquarian booksellers in town, and I think that, among my friends in the avant-garde community, no other literary treasure has grown to become so coveted a possession.

Roo Borson

Glimpses of World History—Jawaharlal Nehru

"I DO NOT KNOW when or where these letters will be published, or whether they will be published at all, for India is a strange land to-day and it is difficult to prophesy." Thus begins *Glimpses of World History,* a volume of collected letters written originally for a single reader, the daughter of Jawaharlal Nehru, by Nehru himself, though it is also easy, with a figure like Nehru, to imagine him writing intimate letters to his daughter all the while feeling History looking over his shoulder—just as it is hard to imagine Virginia Woolf setting down her neat turns of wit in the diaries without Literary History in mind. Nonetheless these "glimpses," being addressed to a single reader, are in effect addressed to every single reader: Nehru takes you by the hand on every page as though you were his little daughter, and shows you the wide world bit by bit, beginning with the beginnings of life on Earth and ending near the ends of the earth, or at least one of its endings: the fearsome politics leading into World War II. The letters were written from various prisons, where Nehru was allowed almost no contact with his family, which accounts for some of the intimacy of the tone; the rest is accounted for not only by fatherly feeling but by Nehru's situation: he was one of the rare figures who, by predilection, intellect and position, was able—literally in the world as well as in words—to compose world history and hand it on to his daughter. He lived, unlike most of us, in a society that he had a hand in shaping; so-called "current events" were intimate to him, and their being so made all of the past, and all possible futures, personal affairs.

The collection of letters was revised for publication, but retains the mood of being spoken lovingly to one person. It is remarkable as a "history" in part because it presupposes no historical knowledge on the part of the reader—meant, as it was, as an educational introduction to the political history of the world for one who had only recently entered it, told in the form of true stories by a father to a daughter. The preface to the original English edition is dated January 1, 1934; the copy I grew up with was published in the US in 1942, bought used, and bears the inscription "Happy New Year, 1947" from my mother to my father, as my family was beginning its post-war life, when I was not yet born, and in a time when "to-day" was not yet written as a single word.

Robert Boyers

Malina—Ingeborg Bachmann

For almost a decade I've been recommending and teaching a book that remains in print but is read by almost no one in the English-speaking countries. Neither is it available in bookstores: not in Cambridge, Massachusetts or Greenwich Village, not in Toronto or Berkeley, California. The "lost classic" is a novel called *Malina*, by the Austrian writer Ingeborg Bachmann, who died in 1973 and is remembered, if at all, as a short-story writer and poet.

Malina is a first-person novel told by an "unknown woman," a writer who is more than a little bit mad and more than a little bit brilliant. She lives with a man named Malina on a nondescript Viennese side-street which happens also to be the address of her sometime-lover Ivan. Nothing she tells us about herself quite explains how she came to be what she is, but we are tempted throughout the novel to suppose that her problems have much to do with men. What makes the novel so refreshing and chastening and surprising is that it never permits us to be comfortable with such a reading. For every suggestion that the unknown woman is a victim of particular men—her father, a lover who bites her shoulder—or of various patriarchal institutions—language, the postal service, pervasive spectres of violence—there are other indications that the woman herself is too smart to blame what she is—or not for very long—on clearly identifiable persons or on one-dimensional "impersonal" factors. When the woman herself says that "Fascism is the first thing in the relation between men and women," she quickly reminds us—and herself—that she says many different things without committing fully to any of them. Often her assertions are so sweeping and hysterical, so exaggerated and without qualification, that it is impossible to suppose that she intends us to believe them. No doubt there is a sense in which she does truly believe that men are a "disease," but she also loves particular men, and we are not surprised to learn that the man named Malina offers her consistently sound advice on how best to defend herself—not only against men, but against her own relentless delusions of weakness and victimization.

Malina is not an easy or comforting book. It is rife with anomaly and grievance, with paradox and hysteria. When it is determined to be positive, to renounce perversity and malice, it mistrusts its own tender sentiments and reverts more or less inevitably to its characteristic accent: a compound of the desperate and the accusatory. Occasionally fabulistic and escapist, the novel is more usually apocalyptic and prophetic.

There are those, in German and Austrian literary circles especially, who think *Malina* a feminist novel, and it does surely have more eccentric and provocative things to say about women than most other books any of us can name, though it gives no support to any position, and advances no ideological premise on which any clear-sighted reader would rely. It seems that Bachmann intends to speak of women generally; her character does attribute to men the things that men do, and to women the propensity to receive and suffer. But the book is full of thwarted dreams and many varieties of sensory assault, and there are compelling passages in the novel that assert the anomalous character of this particular

The Holmes and Meier paperback edition, 1999

woman's experience, the obvious unreliability of her insights. If Bachmann intended her unknown woman to speak for women in general, we wonder, why did she take pains to make her hysterical and repellant, a figure unable—though by no means unwilling—to participate in the ordinary, consoling affairs of her world?

Of course, with a novel like *Malina* there are no easy or certain answers. Bachmann writes with the ferocity and subversive self-doubt of a person who feels herself to be going under and wishes somehow to hang on, though she mistrusts even her own instinct to stay afloat. Her unknown woman subjects everything she touches to mockery or to corrosive disbelief. When she imagines herself—briefly, plausibly—contented, she thinks of her condition as "happy, happy, happy," which is to say absurdly, impossibly, idiotically deluded. Every thought of freedom is immediately associated with the prospect of subjugation, as pleasure is associated at once with suffering, intimacy with dependence. When her friend/lover/protector/tormentor Malina seems to her most intimidating, which is to say, most powerful, even "omniscient," he is also most apt to offer her what she needs to survive. Encouragement, when there is any, comes usually in a form that bespeaks menace, or at least protracted suffering, as in "Here there is only war" or "Just learn a new style of struggle" or "You should now go neither forward nor back."

We are amazed at how deeply these formulations seem to us, quite as they are intended, both terrifying and consoling: terrifying because they eliminate any possibility of a hopefulness based on delusion, and consoling because they derive so entirely from an understanding of the person to whom they are addressed. The unknown woman has spent much of her life wishing to be other than what she is, and has blamed the world and men and "universal prostitution" and herself for her own failure to achieve an equilibrium that, in her most lucid moments, she knows to be spurious and, for her at least, neither possible nor desirable. It is the great achievement of Bachmann's novel to suggest that hope sometimes looks like despair, that the ability to stop willing what cannot be willed is often the most important step in the restoration of sanity and the reassertion of strength. There is nothing in the least programmatic or therapeutic in these discoveries, but they come upon us with the force of genuine revelation. Part "love story," part "detective novel," "epic poem," "opera" and, as one astute critic has observed, "psychoanalytic case study," *Malina* is a singularly rich and troubling work.

Brian Brett

Classics Revisited—Kenneth Rexroth

WHAT IS A CLASSIC? This is a question considered decades ago by the former vaudeville actor and poet, Kenneth Rexroth, in a series of essays begun in 1964 and continued until his death in 1982. The essays were finally compiled in *Classics Revisited* (and its sequel *More Classics Revisited*).

Cheeky and loopy, opinionated and diverse, these brief sallies are the most delicious outline of a literary canon I've ever encountered—mostly because Rexroth didn't intend to outline a canon. Instead, they are an appreciation of the human condition, including everything from the Kalevala to Stendhal to Gilgamesh to Sei Shōnagon. Rexroth was a self-educated man (he called universities "fog factories") who'd broken out of the Eurocentric vision long before the term was invented.

What makes the book so different, so delightful, so unpompous, is Rexroth's crusty common sense and knack for metaphor, as when he discusses Julius Caesar's style: "The simple nouns and verbs carom off each other like billiard balls," or his legendary remark on the prose of Tacitus: "a style like a tray of dental instruments."

Classics Revisited, though now reprinted, is seldom mentioned by today's more academic critics, and good translations of several of the works discussed are also still difficult to find. Outlaw books, old standards, they remain lost in the worst sense.

I first stumbled upon *Classics Revisited* when I was twenty-two years old, broke and broken-hearted, on my way home in the winter of 1972, having fled a doomed love affair in Oaxaca. I arrived in Santa Barbara. The hitchhiking was bad; clusters of hippies were stranded on a road still blooming with sixties strangeness and wild rumours about Route 101, tales of rednecks seeking longhairs to beat up, or victims getting acid slipped into their food and being used for weird sex. And everyone was searching for Nirvana, or at least fun. The full lusciousness of life lay ahead on that road.

Then I saw the phone booth and remembered that the fabled mountain-climbing anarchist poet, Kenneth Rexroth, lived in Santa Barbara. To my amazement, I found his name in the phone book. I dialled the number. A gruff voice answered: "Hello."

"Hello, is this Kenneth Rexroth?"

"Yes."

"My name is Brian Brett. I'm a poet from Canada and I just wanted to phone and tell you I've read your work and admire it."

There was a deadly pause, an embarrassing silence. Finally, that bear of a voice said: "Waaalllllll, c'mon up then."

I stayed for a week. We discussed T'ang dynasty poets, potato peddling, Hermes Trismegistus, vaudeville techniques, Ezra Pound's looniness and brilliance, Kropotkin's theories of mutual aid, Ono Komachi's love life and the failings of the counter culture. Nearly everything he addressed in *Classics Revisited.*

I left with my head in the clouds. So this was literature. Sure, he could be a terrible crank with a hiatus hernia and a tendency to grumble, but behind him was a dream, a world literature full of dignity and indignities, surprises and horrors and magic. An elegant dream, indeed.

My first copy of *Classics Revisited* is long gone now. Dozens borrowed it, anyone with the hunger. I bought several more copies and gave them away. If I was going to define how to look at literature, *Classics Revisited* would be that definition—it's a great core, maybe with the addition of a few translations of aboriginal literatures to round it out. It should be given to every first year university student in every discipline. Freely, the way I was given the generous grace of his home, the chance to sit alone on his porch one night—reading earlier versions of those essays—the doorway to a thrilling world.

At the end of my visit I stood skinny under an overweight backpack, more than a thousand miles ahead of me. I was still full of desire for a lost woman named Goodheart. Rexroth's last, rueful words as he recognized my sadness, caught me off guard. "There's love on every trolley car." He winked at me and shut the door. It was a typical Rexroth line—open to all kinds of interpretations, some ugly and some beautiful, and I certainly lingered on them.

NATALEE CAPLE

Capital of Pain—Paul Éluard

CAPITAL OF PAIN IS A BOOK of surrealist poetry by Paul Éluard. It's a tall, narrow white book that never fits on my shelves properly. I found it in the woody sanctuary of Annex Books on Bathurst, in the winter that my Grandy was dying. The title of the book is lettered in fuchsia over a black line drawing of Paul Éluard's head by Pablo Picasso. Monsieur Éluard bears a resemblance to one of Señor Picasso's ex-wives. The book was printed in Japan and when I first opened the pale, narrow cover I was startled to see the crimson double endpapers beneath the milky french flaps. The endpapers are printed with a bookplate design made by Max Ernst as a gift to Éluard. The bookplate depicts a black entanglement of doves, clashing with opened wings in the centre of the red page between the hand-written words, *Apres moi le sommeil.* I held the pages open for minute after minute. It cost too much and I was poor. So I bought it because it was beautiful, to cheer myself up. I took it home and read it for the first time in bed. I was wearing my green pyjamas. My black cat lay asleep on my chest with her head on my shoulder, and my tortoiseshell cat lay over my legs. It was the middle of the afternoon.

In his preface to the book, translator Richard Weisman describes an "oneiric world" in the middle of Paris dreamt into being by a group of young poets after the First World War. That world disappeared fifty years before *Capital of Pain* was translated into English. The Surrealist System of Imagination transformed many brave young brunettes into great mad children; Paul Éluard spun in the middle of that circle beside André Breton and Louis Aragon.

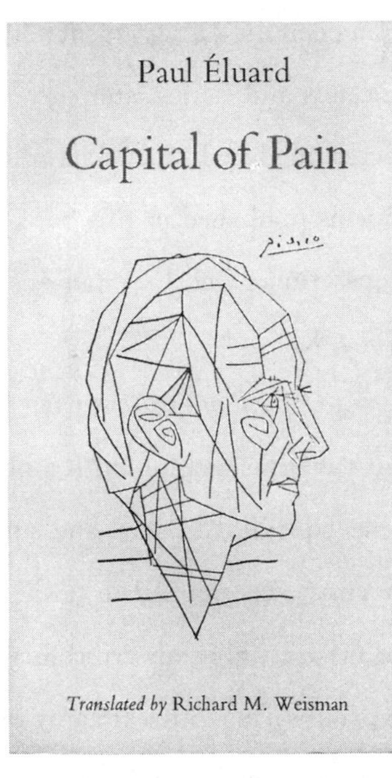

The Mushinsha/Grossman Publishers first edition, 1973

Éluard was eighteen when his first book was published. At the time of its publication he was confined to a Swiss sanitarium for tuberculosis. He met his Russian lover Gala in that sanitarium. He married Gala four years later, concurrent to fighting in the First World War. Éluard was badly wounded by gas during the war. When the fighting was over he and Gala settled in Paris, where he published three more books before he began work on his *Capital of Pain*. In 1924, Éluard disappeared. Rumours of his death turned to resignation. When he finally arrived back in Paris, he explained that he had been on a long journey from Marseilles, through Indonesia, to Ceylon. Friends and critics later surmised that his sudden disappearance had been occasioned by losing Gala to Spanish Surrealist artist, Salvador Dali. Love poems published in this book were written for Gala during their separation: "And I see her and I lose her and I suffer" (from *The Little Just Ones*, X).

Capital of Pain, written between 1921 and 1926, demonstrates Éluard's post-war fascination with a philosophical collapse of the gap between subjects considered trivial and subjects considered grandiose. Éluard writes poems to reason and to faith, to ribbons and to rivers, to monuments and to mouths. He transcribes his unconscious in the Surrealists' automatic writing style, with a dreamy preference for the reality of beauty over the beauty of reality, and for language capable of elaborating meaning over language capable simply of containing meaning.

Russell Smith once told me that although he wrote his Master's thesis on Éluard, he has never seen an English translation of *Capital of Pain*. This exquisite book is considered by many critics to be a seminal text in the surrealist genre, and Éluard's most impressive single volume. Paul Éluard died on November 18, 1952 in Charenton-le-Pont. But on that effulgent afternoon when I first read the lines: "I no longer move silk over the ice / I am ill flowers and pebbles / I love him most inscrutable to the clouds" (from "The Word"), it seemed to me as if Paul Éluard strode into my bedroom to announce that he had just returned from a journey.

Anne Carson

Handbook for William (Liber Manualis)—Dhuoda, translated by Carol Neel

HANDS

Hands are flesh. Handbooks are complications of flesh. Consider Dhuoda's.

About the woman herself not much is known; neither her surname, provenance, nor any reason why her husband should use her so strangely. But her *Handbook* exists and it is one of those pieces of writing that reconcentrates your heart.

Dhuoda was born in (maybe) 804 AD and grew up (somewhere) in the Frankish realm and married a man named Bernard who then banished her (no one knows why) along with their firstborn son to a place called Uzès where she lived out the rest of her life. Bernard was a nephew of Charlemagne and preferred the hot life of the Carolingian court (contemporaries named him the lover of Judith, wife of King Louis the Pious, but

Bernard denied it). His only recorded visit to Dhuoda in Uzès resulted in the birth of a second son. After that Bernard's luck went bad. He fought at Fontenoy on the wrong (Aquitanian) side and then had to pledge faith to the new king by sending a hostage. And so it was that Dhuoda's firstborn son, William, was taken by soldiers out of her hands one cool May morning of 842 and brought from Uzès to the court of Charles the Bald. His mother never saw him again. In November the soldiers returned to Uzès. This time they took her second son, who had no name as he was not yet christened. His mother never saw him again. She wrote the *Handbook* to make sense of these things.

MIRRORS

Tactics of survival for William—both in this world and the next—are the overt subject of her Handbook. She commends him to a twofold gentle service, for he must please the court and also delight God:

> I urge you William, my beautiful beloved son … learn something about God the creator. Implore him, cherish him, love him … But you must also, as written in Job, gird your loins like a man … be greatly glorious and dress splendidly! (Book 1, Chapter 7)

The reference to Job is a little outrageous (if you recall its original thunderous context) as are many of the citations with which Dhuoda's argument is packed and woven. Her learning is a big box where she rummages like a happy Dadaist, splicing Isidore onto Esther onto Ovid, or Prudentius and Pliny with the Book of Psalms. But this method is not a mischief: she is urging William to weave himself a net of safety out of all available resources—pagan and Christian, logical and mystical, worldly and other. Her book is a mirror, she says, where William may look and see what he should do for his mother's sake:

> And when I am gone, you will have this little book of teaching as a reminder: you will be able to look at me still as into a mirror, reading me with your mind and body and praying to God. Then you will see clearly your duty to me. (Book 1, Chapter 6)

His duty is to survive. Mirrors are crucial. Within the mirror of her own Handbook, Dhuoda points to Creation itself as a mirror. Citing Job (12. 7-8), she urges William to consider examples from nature as a guide for his behaviour in the world of men:

> Speak to the earth and it shall answer thee, ask the beasts and they shall

> teach thee and the birds of the air and they shall tell thee and the fish shall tell thee … (Book 3, Chapter 9)

She draws an ideal picture of human society as a "fellowship of reciprocal love" and instructs her son:

> Therefore my son William … in all the changeable situations of the world … cherish and show respect to whatever one or many persons you wish to respect you. (Book 3, Chapter 9)

And from the Roman encyclopaedist Pliny she takes an example of such mutuality:

> Toward our edification in this matter a certain learned author offers a brief comparison from dumb animals … For this is what harts do when groups of them begin to cross seas or wide streams with churning waves—they lower their necks one after the other, each putting his head and horns on the back of the one in front, so that each may rest a little and so more easily cross the current. (Book 3, Chapter 9; cf. Pliny *Natural History* 8.14).

Another mirror of ideal human relations is provided for Dhuoda by language itself. She is writing in Latin and so draws upon the grammar of the Latin language, with an illustration from the Roman grammarian Donatus, as warrant for her vision of reciprocal love:

> Love all and you will be loved by all … if you love them in the singular, they will love you in the plural. It is written in the *Art of Grammar* of the poet Donatus, "I love you and am loved by you, I kiss you and am kissed by you (*osculor te et osculor a te*), I cherish you and am cherished by you, I know you and am known by you." (Book 3, Chapter 9)

Dhuoda is being a little playful in her use of Donatus. *Osculor te et oscular a te* ("I kiss you and am kissed by you") mirrors precisely the kind of fellowship she wants William to practise. For *osculor* is a deponent verb, that is, a verb whose active and passive forms coincide. So, too, in a fully reciprocal love, the beings of lover and beloved may be so deeply fused that no one knows who's kissing whom. She is playing but she is also serious: love of this kind is not unknown to her; at the same time, she hopes such reciprocities may keep William safe amid the changeable situations of the royal court.

And perhaps for Dhuoda the mirror had a further use. I wonder if, gazing into her own looking-glass on long winter evenings in Uzès, she saw her son's face. I wonder if, bending over the pages of her handbook, she felt the two of them were still somehow fused.

ENDS

Clearly she found it all but impossible to break off the writing. Three times in Book 10 she announces an end (*finunt versiculi* ... *finita verba* ... *finit liber*) only to start up again. Even the words

Amen. Dea gratias—

do not prove conclusive: here Dhuoda suddenly remembers she has not asked William to pray for the souls of the dead, so she appends a list of names and then adds her own epitaph, in verse, with the injunction:

Let no one walk away without reading this. (Book 10, Chapter 5)

And still she proceeds to add a postscript (Book 11) on the usefulness of reading the Psalms, before her final citation:

Comsummatus est. (Book 11, Chapter 2; John 19.30)

Hard to let the handbook leave her hands. *Ad me recurrens lugeo* ("reverting to myself I grieve") she says. Yet finally Dhuoda did send the book to her son. Whether or not he read it is uncertain. That he did not take it altogether to heart is demonstrable: arrested in 847, William was executed for treason at the court of Charles the Bald just a few months after his twenty-first birthday. I hope she never knew.

George Elliott Clarke

Play Ebony Play Ivory—Henry Lee Dumas

In 1977, I was 17, stumbling North End Halifax's tumbling, smoky, shabby streets, and being startled into poetry. I had no choice: Halifax was hounding me with its nasty police—their fish-'n'-chip faces, their spraddling eyes—and its dainty, Jim Crow manners. But fierce, Vesuvian voices straight outta Harlem and East St. Louis and South Side Chicago, all those fists-in-the-air Afro-Americans—Sonia Sanchez, Amiri Baraka and Nikki Giovanni—oh yes, all those ain't-scared-a-shit and Black Panther Party poets were just what I needed in a city where it felt like a sin to be black. I had to rage and rage, just to be able to breathe. So, it was the *Revolutionary Young Black Poets*—edited by Ernest L. Coombes—that counted, and none more than Henry Lee Dumas.

But this unknown Dumas, born in Sweet Home, Arkansas, in 1934, and presumably no relation to the famous, nineteenth-century, mixed race

French authors Alexandre Dumas, *père* and *fils*, never appeared in most of the Angry Young Blacks anthologies so chic in the late 1960s. I discovered his poems only because *Play Ebony Play Ivory*, his first book, was stacked with the Coombes anthology on a desolate shelf of black poetry books in the philanthropic Halifax North End Memorial Library, built to honour the dead of the Hiroshima-like Explosion of 1917 and to succour the victims of capitalism. I was drawn to Dumas because the back cover photo of *Play Ebony Play Ivory* revealed a youthful, scholarly, Malcolm X-like face. And I was drawn to him because, like X, he had died violently, bizarrely, by being shot—in a case of "mistaken identity"—by a New York City transit cop in a Harlem subway station—on May 23, 1968. And I was drawn to him because of his beautiful poetry.

Play Ebony Play Ivory is long out of print and quite obscure. But I would never have attempted poetry were it not for that book with its red-bordered, white-print-against-a-black-background cover and its paradise of African-nuanced, Southern-bluesy, Harlem-jazzy, imagist, surrealist, swinging poems. I loved it so much that I photocopied a bunch of the poems on a primitive Xerox, stapled the finished wad of pages together, and then slashed away the excess paper with a jagged-edged paper cutter. The finished "book," about the size of a Penguin paperback, has fantastically ragged edges, a brownish patina, a basementy-smell and a now-rusting staple, but all the pages (save the first) are intact, though I have carried it with great passion across two decades.

I still treasure my pirate version of *Play Ebony Play Ivory*, though a volume of Dumas's selected poetry, *Knees of a Natural Man*, appeared in 1988 from New York's Thunder's Mouth Press and, for all I know (I own a copy purchased in 1989), it may still be in print. But *Play Ebony Play Ivory* is more important because it marked a sable-soft revolution. Here, an African-American poet lyricized black life, without apology, without sentimentality, and without chauvinism. Dumas' contemporaries screamed, "Kill Whitey!" But he, memorializing the negroid King James Version, Bessie Smith, John Coltrane and Otis Redding, sang, instead, "lash/ I take it from you for nothing," and, more positively, "The great god Shango in the African sea/ reached down with palm oil and oozed out me." Radically, Dumas injected an authentic African feeling, via Arkansas, into his poems: "dip with my dipper on the plain of lost reasons/ eons ribbed in pearls."

He penned blues poems, pride songs, all using, to quote another of his lines, "diction in gestures transposed to music." Shamelessly, too, he adorated love: "The trees honor you/ in gold/ and blush when you pass."

Play Ebony Play Ivory be neglected, but Dumas ain't never gonna be negligible. Can I get an amen?

KAREN CONNELLY

The Five Nations—Rudyard Kipling

MY MOTHER TOLD ME the book was priceless. I didn't understand. If something didn't have a price, I thought it must be worth nothing. "No. It means that even money cannot pay for it," she explained. I regarded her with profound eleven-year-old skepticism. If there was one thing I had figured out, it was that money could buy anything, including dusty old books. "But this is a very old book. It would be really hard to find one like it any more. Your great grandfather brought it over from England. That's where all those books come from." And she used the word again, "priceless," to refer to the old books I came to love.

The Five Nations, a book of poetry by Rudyard Kipling, came from the basement bookshelf that sat under an oblong, dust-covered window which spilled oily yellow light in the late afternoons. Those books became the magical attic of my childhood, the place beyond the rest of the house where the past entered me with more peace and sanity than the present.

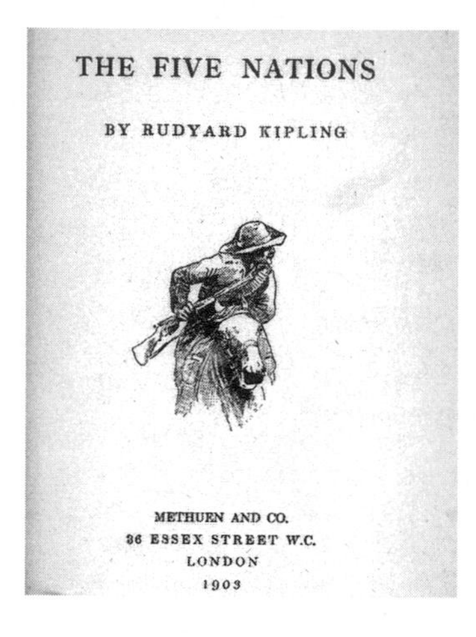
THE FIVE NATIONS

BY RUDYARD KIPLING

METHUEN AND CO.
36 ESSEX STREET W.C.
LONDON
1903

Title page from the Methuen and Co. edition, 1903

The book I loved the most was Kipling's.

After a long struggle involving an English teacher and two dictionaries, the word "priceless" was mine. Invaluable; something so valuable that not even money could buy it. It boggled and delighted my child's mind. I inhaled the heavy yellowed paper, and felt the secret pride of being privy to a miracle. I sat on the top bunk-bed in the room I shared with my sister, holding the red cloth-covered book reverently, stunned with the wonder and perversity of it; I had access to something that was priceless! As a child who never got the nice shoes, or the good clothes, or the new bike, I gloated about my riches beyond riches.

And I read and read. *The Five Nations* was the first book that obsessed me. I thought deeply about Adam-Zad the bear, and the pioneers—depicted by Kipling as well-meaning but crazy—and the Queen, who was clearly far more beautiful than the queen we had on our pennies, and the horses of the war and of the sea. "The White Horses" was the first poem to plunge me into the paradox and power of metaphor. Was Kipling writing of real horses or of the white waves of the sea, so like the rearing horses of the war?

'Twixt tide and tide's returning
Great store of newly dead, —
The bones of those that faced us,
And the hearts of those that fled...

And come they for your calling?
No wit of man may save.
They hear the loosed White Horses
Above your father's grave.
And, kin of those we crippled,
And, sons of those we slew,
Spur down the wild white riders
To school the herds anew.

I memorized these poems and, besides a dozen others by modern poets, they are the only poems I still know by heart. I realize now that the way the stanzas were set up on the page, with marked indentations, deeply influenced the physical shape of my own first book of poetry. The book also contained poems about India and Burma; twenty years later, so far from Kipling, I am writing a book about Burma. One poem I found particularly haunting was "The Old Men":

We shall not acknowledge...
(That the sere bush buds or the desert blooms or
  the ancient well-head dries),
Or any new compass wherewith new men adventure 'neath new skies.

We shall lift up the ropes that constrained our
  youth to bind on our children's hands;
We shall call to the water below the bridges to
  return and replenish our lands;
We shall harness horses (Death's own pale horses)
  and scholarly plough the sands.

At eleven, I thought this was a painfully accurate description of most of my teachers. Kipling seemed visionary to me; he was the first writer to illuminate the strangeness of poetic language. He was the first true poet I'd encountered, and he showed me what poetry could explore: the far-flung world, animals, madness, war, aging, death, the possibility of god and of meaning in an unpredictable world.

Of course, as a child, I was just enthralled, fascinated, freed. And exultant: I understood the meaning of the word "priceless." That knowledge has remained with me all these years, inside me, at the very centre of my life.

Carole Corbeil

Bernadette, French Girl's Annual

When I was ten, my parents gave me a bound collection of French magazines for girls called *Bernadette*. In those days—the Quebec of the early sixties—the only books that came my way, with the exception of history textbooks thick with martyred Jesuits, were French books from France, so that the country of my imagination was very different from the Montreal of my reality. That this is so probably explains why I always experience a kind of luxurious swooning, a coming home to pleasure, when I read stories set in France. In any case, there was a story in *Bernadette* that has stayed with me all my life. And I think it stayed with me because it touched on what made me want to be a writer.

Most of the stories in the annual were illustrated, laid out like comic books, and most of them were historical in nature. I don't remember the title of the story, but it was set in the Second Empire, and it featured three girls who went to school together. The girls were good friends even though they came from different backgrounds. There was a rich, aristocratic girl, a bourgeois girl and a poor girl. The poor girl came from a "genteel" family, but her father had died and her mother was penniless. The girls often talked about the future, and I remember their faces as lovely and pensive beneath their bonnets as they did so. The rich girl and the bourgeois girl wore cloaks, while the poor one had no bonnet and wore a shawl.

Eventually it came time for them to graduate. The girls made a pact to meet again in ten years. They were to turn up on the such and such a corner of a Paris street at a specific time on a specific day. Should they lose touch with one another over the years, they could count on this assured reunion.

I don't remember how the years passed. But I think they passed with history lessons. On Louis Napoleon. On the Franco-Prussian war. The important thing is that years passed and everything changed.

I think the rich girl, whose family had been tied to Louis Napoleon, got poor; the poor girl married a man who inherited a fortune from an uncle; and the bourgeois girl lost her husband to a war in Mexico. The specifics don't matter. What matters is that when you're ten, ten years is a long time. It's the difference between ten years old and twenty years old, and this was my first true understanding of the weight of years. It was like a stab in the heart. After reading the story, I remember feeling this poignant nostalgia for my own life, as I imagined my future self looking back at my ten-year-old self. And as I looked back on my little life, I suddenly became very scared of losing any minute of it, of forgetting anything that had happened. The idea of time passing, of change, of becoming something other than I was, filled me with dread and wonder. Like myself, the girls had had no idea what would become of them. It was so chilling not to know what was coming! And I couldn't get over the sensation of time ruining things. All of this panicked me, but the panic was sweet and sad, and I would deliberately recall it sometimes and loll about in it, as if it were a treat of some kind.

I knew I could address this panic by hoarding my memories, and I did that. Eventually I began writing things down in journals. I spent most of my life memorizing my experience as it was happening so I could write it down in a journal, or collecting my thoughts so they wouldn't disappear. This habit stuns me now.

I suppose anything could have started it, but it was this story in *Bernadette* that triggered nostalgia for life even as it is being lived. I guess that's a kind of definition of literature. In fact, most of the novels I've loved have had this poignant, elegiac quality, and when I close such a novel I often say those words, time passing, and feel that sweet sadness. It's funny, now that I'm older, I care less and less about holding onto the past. These days in my dreams I'm driving cars and the luggage is flying out the back windows. And I don't care. I really don't. Let it all go, I say, except for what comes back, as if from the very marrow of my bones, just before falling asleep.

Robert Creeley

How I Become One of the Invisible—David Rattray

PERHAPS IT IS FINALLY the fact that some people lead interesting lives, but to me the consummate need has been their ability to speak of those lives, to give them an articulate voice and presence. When young, I longed for someone who would talk to me and, often as not, that person was found in a book. Voices as distinct as any physically present really were there—Lawrence's intensity, Conrad's curious particularizations, Stendhal's endlessly relieving humour, all were my dependably familiar company. Long after I lost the literal memory of just what he had said, I still heard Henry Miller talking, displacing all usual discretion, demanding intimacy with his listener.

Just so then is the writer I now think of, given the question of a "lost classic," which, in this case, seems never to have been quite found. David Rattray's book is still in print, though sadly he died in 1993, still with much in mind to do, still decisively able—as his last collection, *Opening the*

Eyelid (1990), makes very clear. He is probably best known as the translator of Antonin Artaud, having done, as he says in this present book, "roughly two-thirds" of Jack Hirschman's edition of Artaud's work, *Anthology*, published in the mid-sixties. (I see now that another instance of his authority as a translator, *Black Mirror: The Selected Poems of Roger Gilbert-Lecomte*, was published posthumously in 1996.)

Rattray's collection of reflections, memoirs and essays, *How I Became One of the Invisible*, published in 1992 by Semiotext(e), is that rare instance of a book in which the writer speaks of the proverbial "many things" of a life, all in a manner which is in no way defined as a professional habit, an authority, an identity given him or her by some public use. Stendhal has such a voice, Montaigne also in a curious way—and Whitman, in his journals especially, or Borges in his fictions. It is as though the writer were attending his or her own experience in company with the reader, were not, that is, explaining or directing, but coming again to the same terms, place and time, as the reader begins then to enter. Robert Duncan was a master of this possibility as were other very different writers, Robert Louis Stevenson, for example, or Francis Parkman. Defoe is its great practitioner in *Robinson Crusoe*. Such address can say anything, go anywhere, and be there so specifically in its own compelling interest that all, the reader included, then follows.

Essays are otherwise a bore, trials, labours, persuasions. The tender homage Rattray writes to his college friend, Alden Van Buskirk, becomes an extraordinary record of the time itself, the last of the fifties, with all its characteristic wandering and hopes. Nothing I've read ever placed it in mind so clearly, or knew to begin with what it had all been about. Just so is the ranging diversity of all this book engaged, whether the poet Faiz Ahmed Faiz (1911–1984) or "a certain ancient type of music which the musicologist Denis Stevens refers to as 'that once mysterious melange of plainsong and polyphony, the "In Nomine" ...'" One reads of Holderlin, of Rene Crevel, of Rattray's brother's death from cancer (which was to be the cause of Rattray's death as well), of Artaud and "the cane's loss of power"—of Emile Nelligan, whom Edmund Wilson called "the Rimbaud and Nerval of French Canada." The final piece, "How I Became One of the Invisible," opens with this paragraph:

> In order to become one of the invisible, I had to go through an ordeal technically known as throwing oneself in the arms of God. This consisted of going out in the empty desert with nothing but the clothes that one was

wearing and a bag containing certain things. Some of us stayed there for months, others years, many forever.

Rattray and I were writing to one another at the end of his life. He had hoped to be able to come up to Buffalo for a reading but his health in the last months prevented it. We talked on the phone from time to time, and I knew in a small way what he was having to deal with. This book I so value told me the rest. It was unexpected counsel for a great deal I myself had come to and would one day have to accept. He sent me a sweet poem dated March 2, 1993:

Eleven bantam eggs

In numbers even
Sang St Stephen
But number odd
Rejoiceth God

Whatever books there have been or will be, it seems to me now that there must be in them a presence such as his was, however it speaks or feels. Who touches this book touches a man, Whitman says—who feels the world, who keeps the faith, who shares with us.

SARAH ELLIS

Beyond the Pawpaw Trees—Palmer Brown

VERY OCCASIONALLY A BOOK falls into one's lap at exactly the right moment. For me, one of these moments occurred halfway through grade four. The divine emissary was the Scholastic Book Club at school. The book was *Beyond the Pawpaw Trees* by Palmer Brown.

How I came to choose this book I don't remember. It wasn't like my usual choices of that period—school story, inspirational biography of a handicapped person or tale of the olden days. But the moment I looked at the cover, with its scratchy drawing of a girl leading a camel across the desert, framed by a border of little objects—book, seashell, pot of gold, hot water bottle, hedgehog, curly-toes slippers—I felt myself going into a room in my head that had always been there, but that I had never before entered. The Goddess of Serendip is like that. She looks beyond surface interests and identity into your very soul.

Beyond the Pawpaw Trees is a road book. At the opening of the story

Anna Lavinia leaves her home and her mother (her father is away chasing rainbows), travelling for the very first time beyond the garden walls, on an expedition to visit her Aunt Sophia Maria. With only her stowaway kitten for company Anna Lavinia sets off by train. In this leg of the journey—a set of gentle encounters—Palmer Brown re-creates the out-of-time, rhythmical, mesmerizing pace of train travel with its concentration on the small affairs of the moment. This act ends when the train reaches the spot on the horizon when the train tracks come together.

By this point all the adults have disappeared and Anna Lavinia, unfazed, continues her journey on foot until she comes to the edge of a steep cliff. In the distance she sees a walled town with "pink and white towers with round tops like onions." Here the flavour of the book changes. We move from the cozy world of kittens, cakes, kindly train conductors and home preserves to Araby—to parrots, turbans, palm trees, silks and the smell of cinnamon. This change is signalled by a change in Anna Lavinia herself. Caught on the top of a cliff, longing for distant and seemingly inaccessible delights, she notices an uprush of warm air; so, after a sensible risk assessment, she simply opens her umbrella and steps off the edge of the cliff. Sure enough, she floats safely to the desert floor.

The distant town contains an hospitable pasha who gives Anna Lavinia a camel. In this mode she crosses the desert, visits an oasis and then, in a town in the middle of a mirage, she finally finds the home of her aunt. In fairly short order she also finds her father, the end of the rainbow and fourteen pots of gold. The family returns home in about a page and there is the completion of the heroic journey, laughing and crying, a couple of songs and a bowl of oatmeal.

When I reread this book as an adult I can almost capture the childhood rightness of it, the way one can almost capture the taste of a dream upon waking. One of the elements of its appeal is and was fascination with the miniature. This is a story of close-ups. It opens with a highly detailed description of trying to thread an uncooperative needle. There is a spyglass and a microscope. The drawings, also by Palmer Brown, are crammed with detail and decoration. This is the engrossing territory of the tiny.

The territory of the pawpaw trees is an odd but winning combination of lush and sensible. The lushness comes from the rosy light of sun shining through jars of pawpaw jelly, dinners by lantern light, and the popping sound of a desert bursting into bloom after a rain. The sensible strain comes from adults who make such comforting pronouncements as "Eat because it is fun," and from Anna Lavinia herself, who, like Carroll's Alice, faces the oddities of her world with courage, courtesy and an earnest desire to make meaning out of confusion. My childhood reading, particularly of those "olden days" books, gave me many female role models of pluckiness: young women who defended their garrison against savages, or pioneer girls who saved their sisters from drowning. Secretly, though, I found Anna Lavinia, with her doughty matter-of-fact determination a more inspiring and more realistic acquaintance.

Those grade four girls are still around, with their fascination for the miniature, their courage, their determination to make sense of the world. They hear the siren call of the open road and they know the sustaining necessity of the familiar hedgehogs of home. This book is for them.

Jeffrey Eugenides

The Pilgrim Hawk—Glenway Wescott

Looking back now—I turn forty next week and this is what happens—it seems to me that many of the stories I liked when I started writing had animals in them. There was the dung beetle of Kafka's *Metamorphosis*. There was the peacock in Flannery O'Connor's "The Displaced Person". (I wasn't the only person who liked that peacock. It turned up, hardly altered, in Raymond Carver's story "Feathers" many years later.) The animals I went for weren't the wild, White Fang variety. The wildlife that appealed to me was also displaced: the exotic peacock to that drab Southern farm; the dung beetle to the baroque city of Prague. The irruption by these animals into the human sphere—which, I suppose, is a central characteristic of myth—created a tension that quickened my interest. It promised an exchange between worlds, not so easily come by in modern fiction. The animals held in their claws or teeth or pincers some truth about God or human nature. Something big, anyway.

All this comes back to me when I try to explain why Glenway Wescott's *The Pilgrim Hawk* captivated me so much the first time I read it. The book is narrated by one Alwyn Tower, whose name will give you some idea of the novel itself: its mandarin tone, drawing room setting and European sensibilities. Tower, an American expatriate, is staying in the house of his "great friend, Alexandra Henry." The house is in France, where sex is sophisticated and mysterious, as is Tower's relationship with Alex. What's he doing in the house alone with an unmarried woman in 1927? Are they really just friends? On the first page we're told that Alexandra later returns to America and marries Tower's brother. This knowledge hangs over the novel, arranging Tower and Alex into two sides of a love triangle that hasn't quite formed. Soon enough, other triangles appear. An Irish couple, the Cullens, arrive with their chauffeur, Ricketts. In the kitchen, preparing dinner, are the Moroccan servants, Jean and Eva. And to complicate matters further, there's the animal: "[Mr. Cullen] turned to help Mrs. Cullen out of the car, which was a delicate operation, for she bore a full-grown hooded falcon on her wrist. A dapper young chauffeur also helped. She was dressed with extreme elegance and she wore the highest heels I ever saw, on which, with one solicitous male at each elbow, she stumbled across the ancient cobblestones, the bird swaying a little and hunching its wings to steady itself."

The bird, obviously, was right up my alley. The arrival of such an outlandish creature into the genteel precincts of Alexandra Henry's house set up just the opposition that I found so compelling in fiction. Wescott's descriptions of the falcon, from its physical appearance to its unappeasable physiology, have the precision of zoological observations. From there he lifts into the register of tragedy—and all by page twenty: "[Mrs. Cullen] informed us, for example, that in a state of nature hawks rarely die of disease; they starve to death. Their eyesight fails; some of their flight feathers break off ... The hungrier they get, the more wearily and weakly they hunt.... Finally what appears to be shame and morbid discouragement overcomes them. They simply sit on the rocks or in a tree somewhere waiting to die, as you might say philosophically, letting themselves die."

The hunger falcons feel isn't like human hunger. It's a far fiercer, more desperate urge. The ferocity of this hunger is what drives these wild animals to make their pact with humans: food in return for captivity. And here we arrive at the novel's theme, or so we think. As Mrs. Cullen (trying not to get blood on the furniture) feeds the hawk a pigeon, Tower reflects on the creature. And I mean reflects. He compares the hawk's appetite to human sexual passion. He likens its captivity—unhappy in many respects, yet one of its own choosing—to marriage. He thinks the way falcons starve to death is similar to the slow wasting away of the failed artist. And on and on. The pilgrim hawk becomes a symbol for everything that is going on around it: Ricketts flirting with the Moroccan girl in the kitchen; Ricketts possibly flirting with Mrs. Cullen; Mr. Cullen salivating for his dinner.

Even with this reading alone, *The Pilgrim Hawk* would deserve longevity. But it's what happens next—what Wescott does next—that takes the book out of the arena of the well-crafted, symbolic story, of the animal tale that invigorates naturalism with a shot of myth, and brings it up to a level I couldn't appreciate at twenty, but which I now associate with a classic, lost or found.

Here is what happens. Near the novel's end, after much commotion (Mr. Cullen either tries to murder Ricketts or kill himself, and a car accident ensues), Mrs. Cullen reappears as she did at the beginning of the book. Once again, she enters Alexandra's house with the bird on her arm. But now something has happened to the animal. "It was absurd", [Tower says]. "Even her little blind headgear with parrot feathers seemed to me absurd; it matched the French hat which her mistress was wearing at so Irish an angle, except that it was provided with secure drawstrings. In spite of my bewilderment and alarm, I began to laugh. It struck me as a completion of the cycle of the afternoon, an end of the sequence of meanings I had been reading into everything, especially Lucy. The all-embracing symbolic bird; primitive image with iron wings and rusty tassels and enameled feet; airy murderess like an angel; young predatory san guinary de luxe hen—now she was funny; she had not seemed funny before."

It's this daring on Wescott's part, the courage to unravel the tapestry of meanings he has laboured so assiduously to weave together, that makes the novel great. Not because it accords with theories of deconstruction; not because it affirms a fashionable skepticism about the limits of human intelligence; but because, in this shifting of meanings, the reader experiences the complexity both of the world and the consciousness through which we perceive it. The pulling of the rug of surety from under the reader's feet is nothing less than what happens to a person proceeding through life.

What I like about *The Pilgrim Hawk* today, then, is something different from what originally attracted me. The displaced animal is still there; the narrative still hooks me in; the sentences are as supple and elegant as ever. But now, in addition to all the clamorous meanings the hawk represents—which by no means are cancelled out by their not being absolute—I find a deeper, sadder truth: the truth of never being able to get to the bottom of it, of any of it. Of love. Of marriage. Of sex. Of this life itself, so full of appetite and thinking.

DOUGLAS FETHERLING

Confessions of an Un-common Attorney—Reginald Hine

REGINALD HINE (1883–1949) was a bookish lawyer and amateur antiquary whose existence I learned of from a friend of mine, a specialist in comparative legal history and legal etymology, who long ago stumbled on Hine's autobiography, *Confessions of an Un-common Attorney*. This is Hine's most popular or perhaps least unheard-of book and so not too terribly difficult to find in a large institutional library. To locate the others, however, might require considerable diligence and luck in some out-of-the-way second-hand bookshop, particularly in the sections where the proprietor's dog likes to sleep, sensing that it won't be disturbed by browsers.

You might find a stray Hine in the section where English-county histories are shelved, for instance, as Hine wrote a number of such works about his native town, Hitchin in Hertfordshire. Or he might turn up in Religion. Although a comparison shopper for spiritual goods, Hine enjoyed writing about the Quakers, with the "silent reproof of their better practice, their sad renunciation of colour, their grey prohibiting outlook on the arts and graces of this present life." You might even find him in Literature (his book on Charles Lamb is still in print).

The height of fortune would be to get your hands on a copy of *The Cream of Curiosity* (1920). Hine was a dedicated book-hunter himself and a friend of many writers, and he formed an important collection of manuscripts, both literary and historical. When the time came to dispose of it, he first set down all the pertinent information about each item, imbuing the references with the style and grace characteristic of his personality.

The operative word is personality. Hine was one of those rare writers, like Sir Izaak Walton, whose work is so attractive because it is the product of a good soul, an upright conscience who genuinely loved his fellow humans, however exasperated they might often be with him and he with them. Such is the voice behind the prose, which the tales he tells merely amplify. His story, in brief, is that around the turn of the century, he articled to a firm of solicitors that had been operating in Hitchin uninterruptedly since Elizabethan times. His discovery, in the attic, of legal papers going back to the beginning is what prompted him to become a local historian, a social one specifically. He became a collector of such documents, as well as of folklore, folk remedies, quotations, and all the other sorts of things people used to enter in their commonplace books. "By his selection from their jotted notes," Richenda Scott wrote in her preface to a posthumous gathering of Hine's essays and articles, "he showed us the inmost problems with which his fellow men and women wrestled ..."

Hine explains the title of his memoirs by pointing out that until midnight, October 31, 1875, when the Judicature Act went into effect, what is now always called a solicitor was usually called an attorney. Under the old system, to tag someone "a common attorney" was to suggest that the person was of the lower legal order, schooled only in the common law and fit for nothing more than "land-jobbing, jerry-building, company-promoting, debt-collecting, writ-serving, time serving ..." Hine was an atypical common attorney in that his life was, by choice, so bound up with the lives of his clients and the community. In his chapter on wills and estates, for instance, he tells of a dying Church of England clergyman who wouldn't allow any girls or women into the room where he lay. It was "a baffling, piteous, rather sinister case, for the client was suffering from the third and last of his strokes, and could neither speak nor move. Yet I could tell from his eyes and from the fumbling of his hands, that he wanted me to find something, or to do something urgently before he died." Between the man's departure from life and the coroner's arrival at the house, Hine made a quick search of the room, turning up a wodge of risqué photos, which he destroyed without a word to anyone. In another passage, he mentions matter-of-factly that one of his clients, an author, left a half-written book at his death. Without any ado, Hine completed the work in the dead man's exact style, then sold it to a publisher to benefit the estate.

Hine says of *Confessions of an Un-common Attorney*, "Truly a book of this character has but one perfect reader, to wit, the author. He [alone] remembers the many delightful but possibly derogatory passages he excised from the manuscript. He recalls the still more inflammable material that lies smouldering in his notes." But Hine does himself an injustice and fools no one in suggesting that he's capable of anything incendiary. Illuminating yes, incendiary never. He enjoyed the law not only because it brought him into contact with people at all the turning points in their lives, but also because "there can be no other profession more apt to kindle and enliven the intellect, and keep a man's reason from rusting." It's typical of him that, as a Victorian and a provincial, he first reacted with horror to

Freud's book *The Interpretation of Dreams*, which a doctor recommended because Hine was a neurasthenic. He actually threw it into the fire. But then he bought another copy and became so deeply absorbed in the subject that he began collecting dreams for study rather than simply noting them for analysis.

The time-worn front panel of the "wrapper" from the Dent fourth impression

Like Thoreau, who said that he had travelled widely in Concord, Hine found the universe in Hitchin. One doesn't need to know or care much about the actual place to understand how perfectly it illustrates how even today the roots of English society go deeply into medieval and post-medieval soil. Despite their narrow focus, Hine's books such as *Hitchin Worthies* are no amateurish local affairs. He spent twenty years writing one of them, ferreting out primary sources as far afield as the Vatican Library. "The study of social history based on careful perusal of local records is comparatively new," Richenda Scott observed shortly after Hine's death.

His achievement, she argued, was that his books "set a new standard not only for the conception and writing of local history but also for the production of such works" in the physical sense, as he was a bibliophile with discriminating tastes in paper and typography.

But most of us would respond to him first for his *scintillae juris* (sorry—Hine's love of Latin phrases is contagious) and for his love of humanity, and for such stories as this one, about J. C. Squire, the important and clever editor and reviewer who's best known today, alas, because Virginia Woolf despised him so. It seems that George Bernard Shaw signed one of his books to Squire "with the Author's compliments," only to discover it years later in a shop in Charing Cross. One morning Squire opened the post to find the book had come back to him like a slow-flying boomerang. There was no note with it, just a second inscription below the first: "To Sir John Squire, with the Author's renewed compliments." Hine is forever a pleasant read. He is particularly therapeutic when you need reminding that—*mirabile dictu*—the world is not so unfriendly as it seems.

Charles Foran

☞

The Third Policeman—Flann O'Brien

Flann O'Brien is twenty-eight in 1939, the year his debut novel, *At-Swim-Two-Birds*, appears. Dylan Thomas is kind to the book in an English newspaper, but otherwise the Luftwaffe and the fall of Paris preoccupy critics and readers alike. Undaunted, O'Brien drafts a second novel in a matter of months and sends it to his London publisher. They pass on the manuscript. The war deepens and neutral Ireland is no one's good friend. Flann O'Brien, pseudonym for Brian O'Nolan, considered the most auspicious literary talent to have emerged from University College, Dublin, since James Joyce, keeps his job as a civil servant. He throws his energies into a newspaper column. He drinks in the company of men who wear white gloves to bars, on account of promises to wives to never touch alcohol.

And the second novel? Lost, O'Brien claims. Over the years, the tale grows more boozy; he is driving at high speed when the manuscript up and flies out the car window, pages strewn across the Irish countryside.

In the late 1950s young editors, stirred by the unbuttoned brilliance of *At-Swim-Two-Birds*, launch a Flann O'Brien revival. Though by then bitter and besotted, he obliges with two more books. Both are funny and show flashes of greatness, but are also cursory, half-realized. O'Brien dies in 1966, a disappointment.

The lost manuscript is found. It is called *The Third Policeman*, and its presence in the author's desk for a quarter-century might well have driven him to drink. The novel is less dazzling than its predecessor but that much more serious and mature: the first draft of a major work. As the years passed and O'Brien further squandered his talents—in a desperate act of secret self-plagiarism, he borrowed bits of it for use in his final novel, *The Dalkey Archive*—the book must have become his own variation on Dorian Gray: a reminder of the writer he once was, or might have been.

Though the "story" behind a novel is never reason enough to read it, *The Third Policeman* benefits from this introduction. Appearing posthumously, and lacking the knee-slapping zaniness of *At-Swim-Two-Birds*, the book has flitted in and out of consideration as part of the Irish canon. It has also been read out of order, so to speak. Many O'Brien fans actually prefer the "lite" work, and cannot fathom the oddness and moral acuity of this manuscript. They think it an aberration, an off-moment.

I believe it is a novel charged with the same weird energy as Thomas Pynchon's *Gravity's Rainbow*. Both deal with the aftermath of a bomb. In Pynchon, the consequence is social derangement; all changed utterly by humanity having bitten into the apple of mass self-destruction. In *The Third Policeman*, the consequence is a narrator transported from his own familiar but deeply strange world into

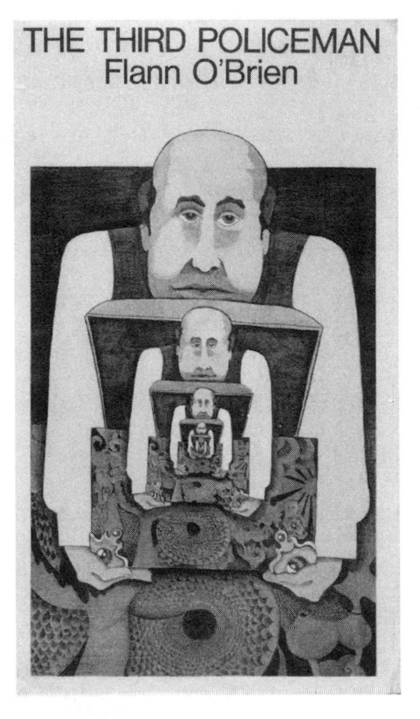

The MacGibbon & Kee edition, 1967. *Design by John Farman*

a parallel one that is strange but deeply familiar. O'Brien invests slapstick and low-brow comedy—a blowhard cop, gags with bicycles and dogs—with overtones of menace. Tall tales turn swiftly dark; the "crack," as the Irish call good banter, starts to crack up. Where we are is Ireland, the book infers—*pace* Marlowe's Faustus on hell—and must ever be.

The Third Policeman is about how our subconscious propels us where our conscious selves wisely refuse to go. It is definitely a parable. It definitely heads down a narrow and dark thematic road. But the novel is also a first draft by an author who shows signs of being disconcerted, perhaps even scared, by what he is creating. (The use of footnotes, supposedly to mock academic pomposity, is a clear hedge.) When I read the book as a graduate student in Dublin I thought it an amazing piece of writing. Few agreed with me. When I did my thesis on the novel, I kept finding more and more there: layers and fears, dares and cop-outs. I couldn't believe so few scholars took the work seriously. In the end, I doubt I convinced many to reconsider.

So the issue of the quality of *The Third Policeman* is far from settled. That doesn't alter the harrowing story of how the novel came into being. Works-in-progress are always precarious. At any moment, the thing can break down. At any moment, you may decide that a month or a year or ten years of effort were for naught. But suppose you finish a book, one that more or less fell out of you, and find it so singular you can't tell if it is brilliant or embarrassing. Suppose you opt to shelve it; suppose you never write anything at that pitch again. Eventually, the abandoned manuscript must start to look strange indeed, ruthless and fanatical, especially compared to your more relaxed, current work. Eventually, you think yourself prudent to have "lost" it. Not a coward at all; an artist much the wiser—and happier?—for knowing his limits and his taste.

HELEN GARNER

The Journey of the Stamp Animals—Phyllis Hay

WHEN I WAS A SMALL CHILD in the 1940s, in a provincial town at the bottom of Australia, there existed in my life a book called *The Journey of the Stamp Animals*. It was the story of four Australian animals who somehow got off the stamps on which they were printed, and set out on a long and difficult pilgrimage—destination forgotten (by me).

Their travels were irresistibly complicated by the fact that each animal was able to eat only things which were the same colour as the stylised stamp-picture of itself that it had escaped from: the kangaroo could eat only yellow things; the sheep, mauve; and so on. (The 'roo could feast on butter, but the poor sheep had to keep searching for obscure things like wisteria, a plant I had not at that stage heard of.)

The book had wonderful illustrations. Most of all I pored over a picture of the Foxy Roadhouse, a sort of nightclub where foxes went to dance.

The four stamp animals, timid creatures with no experience of the world, had to creep past this wicked establishment, whose open doors let fall across the pavement a strip of smoky light. Inside the building, glamorous vixens in tiaras and plunging-necked cocktail gowns were twirling about in the arms of their tuxedoed, snarling partners; and all the foxes' clothes must have had special holes cut at the back, for out of their skirts and trousers gushed great, curved, furry tails. It was an image—sexual, sinister, intensely metropolitan—which thrilled me, as I lay on my bed in my sensible cotton pyjamas, in the humble town of Geelong beside its quiet bay.

But here's the really weird part: except for members of my immediate family, no Australian I've mentioned the book to, in subsequent years, has had any knowledge of it whatsoever. I used to ask people about it all the time, but everyone looked blank. I started to think I must have dreamt it, or that it was a figment of my family's fantasy of itself.

Then ten years ago I wrote a little piece about childhood books for *Vogue* magazine in which I mentioned the mysterious stamp animals and the deep effect they'd had on me. Soon the magazine forwarded to me a letter in trembly writing from an old woman living in a suburb of Sydney. Her granddaughter had spotted my article and brought her the cutting.

Her name was Phyllis Hay. She was excited: she wanted me to know that she was the writer of the book.

It existed! A real Australian person had written it! I was shocked. We corresponded. I asked if she had a spare copy. She said she had only one left, but would lend it to me if I promised to return it. In due course it arrived. I hardly dared to open it. But when I did, out of its battered pages flowed in streams, uncorrupted, the same scary joy it had brought me as a child, before everything in my life had happened. The wisteria was as mauve and as hard to reach, the stamp animals as sweet and determined, the foxes' tails as erotically forceful as I had remembered them. I gloried in the book and in the vindication of my memories. Regretfully, at length, I posted it back.

I heard from its author only once more. She wrote again to tell me that, on the strength of my recommendation, she had suggested to the publisher that they might reissue the book. She was sad to tell me that they had shown no interest at all.

Since then I've found that the library at Sydney University has a copy. I could take a bus and a train and another bus and go and read it—handle it, smell it, look at it—any time I liked. But I never do. I don't want to. I want *The Journey of the Stamp Animals* to be an eternal secret between me and its writer. I don't know if she's still alive. I even managed to keep forgetting her name. Her book is one of those treasures of memory that I have to keep in its own little box, in case it leaks away.

Wayne Grady

❋

Jungle Peace—William Beebe

It wasn't the book I wanted. The book I wanted was *Two Bird Lovers in Mexico*, an account of a trip William Beebe and his wife, Mary Blair Rice, took to Manzanillo just after their marriage in 1902. Robert Henry Welker, Beebe's biographer, describes the Mexico trip as "the first of several journeys which would serve as sources for books, not merely of recorded fact but of personal quest and discovery." Welker says it is not Beebe's best book, but I wanted it anyway, for shortly after we were married, my wife Merilyn and I also spent two weeks in Mexico, not far from Manzanillo, also looking at birds. Every time I went into a used bookstore, and I go into used bookstores as often as Malcolm Lowry went into cantinas, I asked for it. No one had it, no one had seen it, few had even heard of it.

What I found instead was another Beebe book. I was on a science adventure of my own, driving west to work in a dinosaur quarry, part of the research for a book I was writing on the origin of birds. After stopping in Moose Jaw to see some burrowing owls, I dropped down to Eastend to look up Tim Tokaryk, Eastend's resident paleontologist, who had custody of a somewhat mushed-up Tyrannosaurus rex that he and a friend had found a few miles from town. Tim and his wife Norine were also starting a used bookstore, right there in Eastend (paleontologists live on optimism). I offered to help them unpack books and stock shelves for a few days while I picked his brains about birds and dinosaurs.

It was in one of the first boxes: an Everyman's edition of *Jungle Peace*, about Beebe's attempt in 1917 to establish a bird research station deep in the Venezuelan jungle. I read it that night in my van, by candlelight, mainly for his account of hoatzins, those strange, living fossils, technically birds but with two clawed fingers at the tips of thcir wings, thought to be links between dinosaurs and modern birds. Beebe found a colony of them on the Berbice River in what was then British Guiana; he described a nestling hoatzin peering at him from its deep, woven nest: "Higher and higher rose his head, supported on a neck of extraordinary length and thinness. No more than this was needed to mark his absurd resemblance to some strange, extinct reptile."

But long before he got to the hoatzins, I was caught in the intricate

BOOKS BY WILLIAM BEEBE

TWO BIRD-LOVERS IN MEXICO
Houghton, Mifflin Co.—1905
THE BIRD
Henry Holt and Co.—1906
THE LOG OF THE SUN
Henry Holt and Co.—1906
OUR SEARCH FOR A WILDERNESS
Henry Holt and Co.—1910
TROPICAL WILD LIFE
New York Zoological Society—1917
JUNGLE PEACE
Henry Holt and Co.—1918
EDGE OF THE JUNGLE
Henry Holt and Co.—1921
A MONOGRAPH OF THE PHEASANTS
H. F. Witherby and Co.—1918–1922
GALÁPAGOS: WORLD'S END
G. P. Putnam's Sons—1924
JUNGLE DAYS
G. P. Putnam's Sons—1925
THE ARCTURUS ADVENTURE
G. P. Putnam's Sons—1926
PHEASANTS: THEIR LIVES AND HOMES
Doubleday, Page & Co.—1926
PHEASANT JUNGLES
G. P. Putnam's Sons—1927

Detail from the "books by" page in Beebe's Galápagos, *1924 (G.P. Putnam's Sons)*

weave of Beebe's writing, for he was as interested in people and language as he was in birds. When his ship stopped in Martinique, he found it "filled with a subdued hum" of human voices, "a communal tongue, lacking individual words, accent and grammar, and yet containing the essence of a hundred little arguments, soliloquies, pleadings, offers and refusals." On Barbados, during an eclipse of the sun, he observed how, when "walking beneath the shade of dense tropical foliage, the hosts of specks of sunlight sifting through, reflected on the white limestone, were in reality thousands of tiny representations of the sun's disk incised with the segment of the silhouetted moon, but reversed, like the image through the aperture of a pinhole camera."

In Berbice, a quiet, tropical town at the end of the Pomeroon Trail, he spent his days wading through red tape in Colony House and his nights at "the club, the usual colonial institution where one may play bridge or billiards, drink swizzles, or read war telegrams delayed in transit." One night after dinner the stewart approached him timidly: "Would the sahib like to see the library?" He was led up flights of protesting stairs to an upper room, "barnlike in its vacantness," its walls lined with books. "There was an atmosphere about the room which took hold of me at once … something subtle, something which had to discover itself." As he nosed his way along the dustless shelves, each volume in its place and aligned with perfect precision, "the secret of the place came to me: it was a library of the past, a dead library." No one used it, no books had been added to it for years, "most of them were old, old tomes richly bound in leather and tree calf." Among the first-edition Dickens and the colonial reports were little-known histories and charmingly naive reminiscences: *Lives of the Lindsays* and *The Colloquies of Edward Osborne, Citizen and Clothmaker of London.*

He selected a book to take back to his room, turned out the light, then paused for a moment to look about. "The platinum wires still glowed dully, and weak moonlight now filled the room with a silver greyness," and he wondered whether, "in the magic of some of these tropical nights, when the last ball had been pocketed and the last swizzle drunk belowstairs, some of the book-lovers of olden times, who had read these volumes and turned down the creased pages, did not return and again laugh and cry over them. Such gentlefolk as came," he wrote, "could have sat there and listened to the crickets and the occasional cry of a distant heron, and have been untroubled by the consciousness of any passage of time."

And I wondered, as I blew out my candle at the eastern edge of the Cypress Hills and watched nighthawks gliding ghostily over the shortgrass prairie, whether I might some day find myself at the end of the Pomeroon Trail, also looking for hoatzins, and discover that Beebe, before he left Berbice, had slipped back up those creaking stairs to that upper mausoleum, and quietly slid between two long-untouched volumes a copy of his own lost classic, *Two Bird Lovers in Mexico*.

GITHA HARIHARAN

All About H. Hatterr—G. V. Desani

I WAS NINETEEN YEARS OLD when I discovered that I was among the victims of a large-scale burglary. Classics in a range of languages from Sanskrit to Tamil, classics which brought together awesome myths and earthbound tales, classics which would help connect past and present: all these were more or less lost to me even before I knew they were mine. A few, the *Ramayana*, the *Mahabharata* or *The Thousand and One Nights* were familiar, but only as the fables of childhood. They were merely eating-time stories, bedtime stories, too accessible, too local, to be classics.

As I said, I was nineteen; for years I had been indoctrinated in the honour list of classics. As proof, I had just received a degree ("BA Honours") in English Literature from Bombay University. My teachers, a dedicated lot, had done their best. But despite their efforts, I was left with the unhappy conclusion that the "real" classics lived in a distant place. Between their home and mine stood insurmountable geographical obstacles. The makers of the classical canon, the pundits of Great Literature, never looked like us, spoke like us, or ate things we did. What they wrote became classics because they were "European," mostly English. (The Americans got only an endnote or two.)

So in 1974, emerging from the safe (all-women) portals of Bombay University's Sophia College, I had to acknowledge a subversive suspicion. In the real world, literary life did not begin with Chaucer or end with T. S. Eliot. My friends and I took to ransacking the lost-and-found bookstalls of this real world, and read what we could find of that other, unmentionable baggage of classics. Thanks to Macaulay and Co., we had to look for English translations. *The Thousand and One Nights*, for example, came back to us via Burton or the Penguin Classics. (We didn't know then that in the India of the nineties, our lost and found classics would be under threat once more, this time from Hindu fundamentalists.)

But in those days of innocence and discovery, I also stumbled on books in English by non-English authors. They took me far from the classrooms I knew, but not far enough. Then I came across a strange and wonderful book, a novel called *All About H. Hatterr* by G. V. Desani.

All About H. Hatterr is a quicksilver-tongued "autobiographical" of an

Anglo-Indian seeking wisdom from the "seven sages of India." The language swells and flows in torrents, but its originality is tempered with a carefully designed structure. If Hatterr, the eponymous hero, takes the reader on a wild roller-coaster ride, the "entire holus-bolus" has a Desani in masterful control.

When I first read *Hatterr*, I immediately knew it was an important book. But a classic? I mean, is it allowed? Can a classic be so funny, make a fine art of standing Classical Language on its venerable English head? Can a classic be written by a "fifty-fifty," starring a hybrid hero, cooking up a dish of kichdi, the eclectic, nourishing, do-it-yourself subcontinental stew?

All About H. Hatterr, Desani's only novel, first appeared in 1948. It went into a second printing in the second week of publication, and revised editions were published in 1951, 1970 and 1972. The 1972 edition, which is what I have, has a warm and admiring introduction by Anthony Burgess. Desani's novel managed to get the visa required for writers with strange names to travel in the English-speaking world. It attracted praise from the likes of my old BA Honours guru, T. S. Eliot, who said, "In all my experience, I have not met with anything quite like it. It is amazing that anyone should be able to sustain a piece of work in this style and tempo at such length." But possibly because of its resistance to being classified, the novel disappeared from the limelight. It is now, as far as I know, out of print. Though the novel remains a treat to the cognoscenti, and though Salman Rushdie has acknowledged that he "learnt a thing or two" from Desani's bag of tricks, the book remains underground.

Clearly, Desani was aware that his creation was, and would remain, an oddball. This self-reflexive quality is one of the delights of the novel:

> *Indian middle-man* (to Author): Sir, if you do not identify your composition a novel, how then do we itemise it? Sir, the rank and file is entitled to know.
>
> *Author* (to Indian middle-man): Sir, I identify it as a *gesture*. Sir, the rank and file is entitled to know.
>
> *Indian middle-man* (to Author): Sir, there is no immediate demand for *gestures*. There is immediate demand for novels. Sir, we are literary agents not free agents.
>
> *Author* (to Indian middle-man): Sir, I identify it a novel. Sir, itemise it accordingly.

Diana Hartog

Quest for Sita

In the scant library of my childhood home there were no histories, no novels—not even *Reader's Digest Condensed*; no biographies or autobiographies, no links to the outside world beyond the woods that surrounded us. *Autobiography of a Yogi* scarcely counts, since it leaned against other like-minded books which counted as quack esoterica in the 1950s—books on health such as *Back to Eden*, banned from the mails due to some heavy leaning by the American Medical Association.

How the slim red volume titled *Quest for Sita* ended up on that narrow shelf I don't know, and never asked. Its contents were mysterious and sexual, this I knew from its drawings: line drawings of a woman naked from the waist up; a man who carried a bow; and a monkey-man—but all on their separate pages as I leafed through the book at age six. Sita was my secret. Surely my mother had forgotten the book was there, for she always shrugged away any amorous advance by my father; as for my father knowing what was held between the book's faded red boards, no book ever opened upon his lap, only the newspaper.

The book's originally red boards were mottled pink in places; perhaps water figured in its past. If so, *Quest for Sita* had suffered only a sprinkle. It opened cleanly, to cream-coloured paper. Everything about the physical book was clear, the type clear and increasingly legible as I learned to read. I could sound out most of the words, except some of the long foreign ones. The name Rama was easy, as was Sita—she had only that one name, and was beautiful in a strange, stylized way. Her hands lifted in strange gestures, her fingers slenderly pointed and flexible as lizards. It was difficult to know whether Sita was fleeing or merely lost. What was clear was that the Prince was in pursuit. He wanted Sita: I knew this from the drawings, before I even got tangled up in the story. In every picture of her, Sita's breasts faced this way, or that way, as if in disdain at being followed so closely.

I looked up "quest" in the dictionary at school: *a search or the act of seeking*. The tips of Sita's fingers arching backwards. The nipples of her high breasts inscrutable, tiny circles within circles. The act of being sought.

When I left home, I took the book with me without asking permission. I stole it, relying on the principle that whosoever loves a book best is its true owner. But my first lover (after the other first one, who didn't count), my first lover—the one who taught me to follow him places—seemed to think that *he* was the reader most deserving of *Sita*. I showed it to him, loaning it to him at his request, flattered by his interest; and then he disappeared. I would sometimes see him on campus, but he was always hurrying to a class; I'd mention the book, and he'd promise to return it, yes, but he had to run. When we'd briefly been lovers his name had been Steve White, and I'd been sure that he would return my precious stolen book. But then with heightened political awareness on campus he changed his name to Estaben Blanco, the Spanish version, and I was never to see the book again.

I have tried to find it; I have tried to find Estaben Blanco, but there are too many in the San Francisco phone book. In Toronto once I inquired at a shop of rare and used books, but was met with a shake of the head.

I know now that Sita was the fate of Prince Rama in the great epic poem of India, the *Ramayana*. And although I don't know the author of the brief prose version called *Quest for Sita*, I have recently learned that its drawings were executed by the celebrated Mervyn Peake, of the *Gormenghast Trilogy*—an unforgotten classic. This fact makes me a little soft on Peake, that he had it in him, those drawings. Elegant and erotic, they awakened me to their own mystery, and further, to the mystery of the surrounding words.

STEVEN HEIGHTON

The Greenlanders—Jane Smiley

JANE SMILEY'S NAME DOESN'T leap to mind when you try to think of authors whose books have been "lost." Her novel *A Thousand Acres* won both the Pulitzer Prize and the National Book Critics Circle Award for 1991; her books have been bestsellers, have appeared in translation, have been filmed. And yet her superb epic novel *The Greenlanders*, first published by Knopf in 1988, is almost impossible to find, and I've hardly met anyone—even among those who know her other books—who has heard of it, let alone read it. An exception is the Canadian novelist Joan Clark, who recommended the book to me after reading it while writing her own historical novel, *Eriksdottir*.

My encounter with *The Greenlanders* was as painful as it was inspiring. To explain, I have to go back to the mid-eighties when I was trying to finish a BA in English Literature. At that time, at least at my school, there was still a recourse for students hoping to dodge the full-year credit in criticism and theory which is now, I think, mandatory. What I wanted then was to be reading poetry and fiction while trying urgently to write my own, not to be pondering critical theories. And I was not put off, in fact I was intrigued, by the apparently punitive, token alternative offered on the syllabus: Old Norse 310.

So I and another student—a laconic, lanky post-grad with wire-frame spectacles and Einstein hair—met the professor of Old Norse weekly in his cubicle of an office made even narrower by shelves full of fat, calf-bound Eddas, Icelandic grammars, dictionaries and bibliographies. The tiny window behind the desk was occluded by ramparts of old books and papers stacked high on the sill. The professor with his blue eyes, wind-burned face, spindrift silver locks and flowing patriarchal beard might have been standing watch back of the dragon prow of a stormblown Viking ship, while he spent the hour reminiscing about sabbaticals in Iceland and paraphrasing old Norse sagas. At the end of each session he would hand us a rough photocopy of a till-now untranslated saga or poem and wish us luck.

I loved the course. With the help of a dictionary the translations were not too arduous, and I found that along with the expected sanguinary mayhem, many of the sagas showcased a surprising, deadly dry wit. At the same time I learned of the Norse civilization founded by Erik the Red in southwest Greenland just over a millennium ago. Before long I was reading whatever I could find on the topic. There wasn't much. The colony had flourished and spread and at its height had comprised two settlements and some five thousand people, with a cathedral, a bishop sent from Norway, and a proto-democratic annual parliament, as in Iceland at the time. But by the mid-1300s the colony had begun following the climate into decline, after 1430 all trade with Norway ceased, and a century later when the next vessel got through, nothing was left but empty ruined farmsteads and, allegedly, a lone unburied body—the last Greenlander? Despite

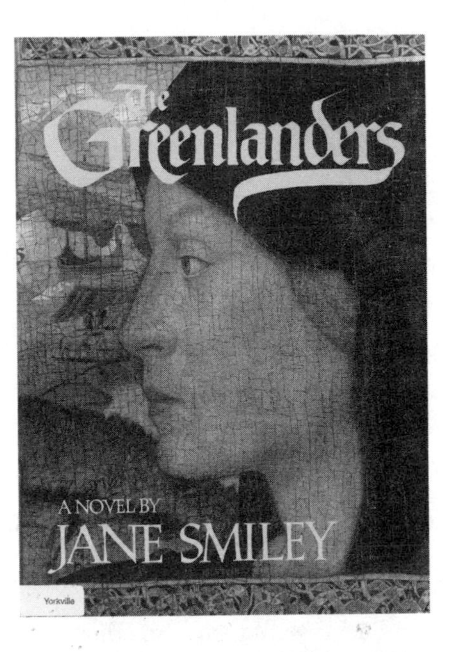

Front jacket of the Knopf edition, 1988. Illustration by John Rush, calligraphy by Gun Larson, design by Carol Devine Carson

all the evidence pointing to climatic change, possible diseases brought by traders, deforestation, inbreeding, conflict with the Inuit or marauding freebooters, the colony's final extinction remains mysterious, as it must. But what seemed clear to me as I read was that large-scale human problems do not change much. The Greenlanders on their lonely, exhaustible chunk of rock, like humanity on the planet, made a microcosm, and their gradual apocalypse was as pertinent as it was poignant. Their story was a modern one in the way that every true story is modern.

So I roughed out plans. My novel of the Greenlanders would have to be epic in length and scope, written in the sweeping chronicle style of the sagas and with the same fusion of elemental drama and wry, resigned humour. It would shun any dungeon-and-dragonish antiquity of style yet still convey through rhythm, syntax and detail a sense of otherness and lost time. It would avoid those obvious anachronisms of sensibility that stultify so much historical fiction. It would have a trans-generational purview comprising love stories, intrigue, dramas of revenge and sagas of survival covering the last century of the colonies for which we have records. It would be, in fact, a book almost exactly like Jane Smiley's *The Greenlanders*—the reading of which was my one experience of finding my own nagging, daunting, untranslatable vision of a book already rendered into words. So that my long-deferred plans were suddenly redundant.

Because of its length, combined with its remote and challenging subject matter, this brilliant novel will likely slumber on in the shadows. Were it not for Smiley's fame it might now be unobtainable except in the occasional second-hand bookstore. But its obscurity, though undeserved, is for me also selfishly gratifying; in some small way, whenever I take it down to reread a few pages, I can still imagine it as mine.

MICHAEL HELM

They Feed They Lion—Philip Levine

A FEW LINES OF POETRY in a book or magazine—though nothing pressed on you, nothing you've been prepared for—cast your way like the glance of the dream-love to the dreamer. There on the page, something changes your consciousness *of* the page. No longer looking down at a thing held open, you're suddenly unsheltered, exposed to the heart of the matter, as if hearing for the first time the word we mean to say when we say "yes."

When the world takes its place again, altered somehow, if you live where I do, you go bookstoring the way others go hunting or clubbing: hopeful, wondering if you can still get lucky.

Once I got lucky with Philip Levine. At this distance I don't remember the lines that won me or where I came across them, but that same day in a used bookstore I found one early volume, took it from the shelf and inspected it with the intensity of a kid with a new comic book. There was Levine's name—until then he'd been just another poet I hadn't read; there was the cover photo, a detail from a ninth-century Assyrian relief, the credit informed me, of a lion penetrated by arrows; and inside the front cover was the handscrawled name of the last owner, a local poet who no doubt had tossed the pearl from the maw of debt. But then, like other rare things, poetry is best passed hand to hand. And anyway, it was a book to be found in person, not asked for by title.

They Feed They Lion. If ever a thing was doomed at the moment of its naming. The title of Levine's fifth volume of poetry should have assured its eventual loss after a short life of being misheard, misordered, miscatalogued. But my 1972 Atheneum edition was the fifth in five years, which suggests that the book bore its burden well. What killed it was what kills so many of the great poets' early volumes—selectedness. (As I write, I've learned that Knopf has just reissued *They Feed They Lion* and Levine's seventh volume, *The Names of the Lost*, in a single volume, though the Assyrian lion has not survived.)

Only twelve of *They Feed They Lion*'s twenty-six poems were included in Levine's *New Selected Poems*. Left out are not only some wonderful pieces, but the whole volume in the sense of a particular world particularly contained.

Here Levine plays variations on a narrow, often seven-syllable line that falls differently every time into a tactile language, hard, heavy, often cold.

The poems are not so much urban as modern. The seventy-six pages hold a lot of violence ("The Children's Crusade"), its portents ("How Much Can It Hurt?") and its aftermath (the title poem, written after the '68 riots in Detroit). They also contain some of Levine's best poems about the working life, especially "Detroit Grease Shop Poem" and "Angel Butcher." We meet the body at work, labouring and aware. We have the sense of poems proceeding not from imagination, or even memory, which is a trick of the mind, but from remembrance, a state of the being. Levine's poems show up so much of contemporary literature as lacking a breadth of experience. The lives in these poems are not only intimate but various, and together they lend the book an unusual amplitude.

As for the mind at work, whatever his subjects—social, personal, political—Levine is physical without lapsing into the tired anti-intellectualism that is still a trap for some American writers lured by what Philip Rahv long ago called "the cult of experience." In Levine's lines there's evidence of exactly what Olson and Williams point to as the blood of poetry.

Not thoughts, but the *play* of thought. The play is endlessly inventive, but it comes down to a poet who shatters all expected things with an image, a line break, a phrasing, as in the movement from the prosaic to the poetic, from the sentential to the linear, effected at times simply by the decision to withhold a preposition or article.

This stanza opens "The Space We Live":

Light shrugs at the last dreams
of cops and whores. The three cold stacks
above the tire factory climb
the dawn. An old man, home from work,
sits on the bed, unlacing.
How small the space a man lives,
elbows on guard, the fingers
curled, the head tucked.

From “Dark Rings”:

Heart of the cottonwood
I chopped in October. The red ants
streaming away from the face
of the axe. A dark soft year,
I trace it with my finger, a year
when the grasses turned
downward and poured into
the roots, a year still
in the white yielding heart.

The poems are funny, necessary, sad, perfectly strange. Whatever its place in our times, the best poetry often seems like the last worthwhile form of public utterance. When it’s lost, the mundane encroaches without making the smallest claim on our attention. But regained, in a bit of chance mixed with faith, though nothing’s forgotten, nothing is familiar.

Greg Hollingshead

Life of Monsieur de Molière—Mikhail Bulgakov

A BOOK I LOVE that I don't see very often, and that few people I mention it to have heard of, is Mikhail Bulgakov's *Life of Monsieur de Molière*. The manuscript is dated 1932–33, but it was not published until 1962, twenty-two years after Bulgakov's death. In America it wasn't published until 1970, thirty years after his death. The edition I have is a 1986 New Directions paperback, the translation by Mirra Ginsburg, who provides a good, short preface. Apparently this translation was published the same year in Canada by Penguin, but I have never seen the Penguin edition.

It was Bulgakov who said, "The artist must love his subject," and his own love for Molière is manifest on every page of the *Life*: love so great as to enable him, in his spontaneous, naked, enthusiastic way, to be fully present to the reader at the same time as he provides a vividly lit, completely authentic and yet uncluttered-by-research account of Molière and his troupe of actors moving through Paris and the countryside of seventeenth-century France. Here, to choose a passage at random, is Bulgakov on the failure of Molière's *Jealous Prince*:

> The public prepared itself eagerly to view Monsieur de Molière's new work, and listened with benevolent attention to Elvire's first monologue, delivered by Marquise-Thérèse du Parc. Then the Prince appeared and began his flowery monologues about glorious dangers, Donna Elvire's shining eyes, and other elevated subjects. The monologues were so long that the audience found ample time for an unhurried examination of the azure sky and gilded loges of the Palais Royal. Molière played on but his heart was uneasy ...

This is less like a biography than a novel filled with surprises, gaps, asides, buffoonery and spare elegance. Molière the subject is a human marvel, deserving and receiving from his biographer kindness and sympathy and a merciless eye. In some ways the *Life* reads like a treatment for a play. Here is Bulgakov on Molière:

> The man stutters and breathes improperly when he speaks. I can also see that

he is quick-tempered and subject to abrupt changes of mood. He easily passes from moments of gaiety to moments of dark reflection. He finds ridiculous traits in men and likes to make them the butt of his jests.

On occasion he carelessly slips into frankness. At other times he tries to be secretive and cunning. He can be recklessly brave, but he can also shift within the moment to irresolution and cowardice. You must agree with me that with these characteristics he will not have an easy life, and will make many enemies! But let him live his life!

By 1930 Bulgakov, whose works met consistently with criticism, censure and abuse, had been barred by the Stalinist regime from all publication and all production for the stage. *Life of Monsieur de Molière* was written by a writer who should have been without hope, a writer who yet was continuing to write, for—as Woland in Bulgakov's cosmically glorious comic masterpiece *The Master and Margarita* puts it—"Manuscripts don't burn." Here is what the author of *Life of Monsieur de Molière* says about the banning of *Tartuffe*: "And what did the author of the luckless play do? Did he burn it? Or hide it? No … the unrepentant playwright sat down to write the fourth and fifth acts." Thirty pages later, Bulgakov asks, "Who can illuminate the tortuous paths of a comedian's life? Who will explain to me why a play that could not be performed in 1664 and 1667 could be performed in 1669?"

The answer is that only the true comedian, who must know those paths so well, can explain such mysteries. I love Bulgakov's courage and generosity and emotional accuracy, and I love his utter lack of pretension. When I read *Life of Monsieur de Molière* he makes me feel for him and his enterprise what he so clearly lets us know he feels for Molière.

Anne Holzman

Reweaving the Web of Life—New Society Publishers

My sister and I fantasized a conspiracy for this book. We would cover the mid-Atlantic states (she took New York, I got the rest), buying up the remaining copies so that there would be a hefty supply for future generations of lefty activists. The only trouble was that like all the other activists we knew, we both moved once a year, and our parents had long since tired of managing our stuff. The conspiracy remained a fantasy.

I even went so far as to lose my own last copy of the book. After a weekend in a midwestern town training a Witness for Peace/Habitat for Humanity delegation for a trip somewhere in Central America, I left my copy of the precious book at the host's home. The host brought it several months later to the city in which I lived, where he left it with a fellow lefty activist. But several months is several months, and once again I had moved on. I heard about this weeks afterwards from yet another lefty activist, but somehow I never made it back to claim the book. I think of the book often, wondering what it would take, how many activists in how many countries I would have to visit by now in order to recover my copy.

The book is *Reweaving the Web of Life*, published several decades ago by New Society Publishers. During my brief stint managing a bookstore in Washington, DC, I heard from the publisher that they were almost out of copies and would not be reprinting it. I argued but to no avail. The situation induced a rare panic in my otherwise keep-rolling-and-gather-no-moss approach to life. I had delegations to train, church services to plan and lead, and plenty of other activities that required the short, imaginative and carefully edited contents of that generous tome. Given how often I either lose a book or hand it over to someone who needs it more than I do, I began to despair. And with good reason. Seasons and cities later, another training assignment found me up the creek without my customary paddle, and the book out of print. How many times, as an activist, an English teacher, a student, have I longed for the rich variety of that book!

This is one of those stories that ends with the protagonist wandering around in the wilderness: in this case an interminable series of used bookstores. I fantasize now that someone else had the same idea my sister and I had, only they had a basement and still live in the same house, and that one of these days I'll get invited to dinner and the host will say, "By the way, we've got a whole case of *Reweaving the Web of Life* downstairs gathering dust. Anybody need a copy?"

Isabel Huggan

Islandia—Austin Tappan Wright

Frankly, revealing my early taste in novels is a little embarrassing, perhaps because the book in question is one I can no longer comfortably read, the prose too rich for my palate. (I find other girlhood favourites such as Lawrence or Durrell equally indigestible, possibly as a result of aging: older people can't handle excess the way the young do.)

Still, I am compelled to be honest and admit that *Islandia*, read in my early twenties, has stayed with me and remained a "place" in my interior landscape. This doesn't mean it is a great book, however: even when I bought it in the 1960s, the paperback version—a hefty 940 pages—was labelled by the publisher an "underground classic," a sure indication of anticipated obscurity.

Written by Austin Tappan Wright and published by Holt, Rinehart and Winston Inc. in 1942, *Islandia* is a utopian romance, perfectly realistic in its history and geography, its social and political detail. I was taken by its semi-philosophic, socio-critical message (anti-American enough to be nicely satisfying), its richly layered plot structure, and the winning nature of its protagonist, John Lang, a young American sent out in 1901 as consul to the country called Islandia on the Karain subcontinent in the Southern Hemisphere (somewhere in that huge oceanic space beneath India and between Africa and Australia, I believe). Wright developed his many characters fully and lovingly, so that *Islandia* is not only a document about Lang's adventures, romances and moral choices, but also about the people with whom he comes in contact and among whom he decides to stay.

Interior map illustration (detail) from the Signet paperback edition, 1958

But the major reason I find *Islandia* worth mentioning here is that it did for me what any good book should do. It transported me. I was taken into its pages, I achieved that intense "sense of place" you find in Faulkner or Munro. It felt real: I have no higher praise for words on paper.

Islandia is still for me a physical reference point. There are times when, in my travels, I will come upon a scene and think, "Ah, the marshes of Dorn Island," or "Heavens, we're at the Vaba Pass." Somehow, the land and sea and sky of the novel impressed themselves into my consciousness as firmly as if I had experienced them, so that they still reside there as templates. There's a cove along the coastline of Quinte Isle in Ontario I first saw in the 1970s with a frisson of recognition—I knew I had already skimmed along that shore with Lang and Dorna in her sailboat *The Marsh Duck*.

Another aspect of the novel which lingers are several Islandian concepts which I found, at the tender age of twenty-two, to give voice to my own thoughts: several words for love, for example, in the manner of the Greeks, making fine distinctions amongst *amia*, friendship; *apia*, sexual desire; and *ania*, the choosing of a marital partner. One notion in particular has stayed in my vocabulary all these many years later: *tanrydoon*. This pleasant-sounding word denotes the setting aside of a room in your house, to be prepared at all times for the visit of a friend who is as close to your heart as if related by blood. A much more specific application than "guest room," *tanrydoon* is an honour bestowed on a person who will now have, for the rest of time, a place in your home.

The only other person I know who has read *Islandia* cover to cover is a woman named Molly to whom I lent it during the first flush of book-love. Quite taken with the romantic sweep of the novel, she decided to name the family farm *tanrydoon* and hired an Irish friend to paint a wooden sign to hang on the mailbox. Unsurprisingly, given his Celtic turn of mind, he doubled the "n" and invented TANNRYDOON, which somehow seemed just right. Until Molly's death a few years ago, that sign hung at the end of her lane as a visible reminder of the transformative power of language, and the joy to be had in passing on books we love.

Laird Hunt

Some Chinese Ghosts—Lafcadio Hearn

Curiously, it is a book I haven't read. I saw a copy once: a dark blue, leather-bound Modern Library edition that sat unread on my girlfriend's uncle's shelf. It was all I could do (i.e., my girlfriend said, No!) not to steal it. I have loved Lafcadio Hearn's writing since my introduction some eight or nine years ago in Japan via a friend's vivid recounting of two of the weird and lovely tales ("Mimi Nashi Hoichi" and "Yuki Onna") that make up his most famous book, *Kwaidan*, a work that I quickly purchased and quickly—largely in hopes of assimilating its peculiarly effective blend of quaintness and ferocity—devoured. Some writers one reads to saturation, to exhaustion; others are taken in brief, startling doses. For me, Hearn falls among the latter. Which is to say that if I have loved Hearn, I have also, for considerable periods of time, not read him, and that each unlooked-for rediscovery (*Glimpses of Unfamiliar Japan*, *Gleanings in Buddha-Fields*) has been invigorating, strange, good. But that is only part of the reason why every time I go into a used bookstore I check to see if they have the above-mentioned edition of *Some Chinese Ghosts*.

In Borges' great story, "Tlön, Uqbar, Orbis Tertius," he writes of a certain class of objects, very rare, that are brought into being by hope. When I walked into my girlfriend's uncle's living room, I had very much been hoping, as we drove down from Vermont and into Massachusetts—excellent used bookstore country—to encounter a slim, elegantly bound edition of stories by Hearn of the same otherworldly stamp as *Kwaidan*. And there, of a sudden, it was. Two other times I have experienced something like this. The first time, on my birthday a few years ago, I went to the Strand bookstore in New York hoping (I had no idea whether or not such a thing existed) to find a small hardback copy of Kafka's parables, perhaps, I

LEAVES FROM THE DIARY
OF AN IMPRESSIONIST
CREOLE SKETCHES
AND
SOME CHINESE GHOSTS

BY
LAFCADIO HEARN

BOSTON AND NEW YORK
HOUGHTON MIFFLIN COMPANY
MDCCCCXXII

Title page from the Houghton Mifflin Company "large-paper" edition, 1922

pictured it, bound in red. After searching that over-heated chaos of stacks and shelves and turning up only a dog-eared copy of the selected stories, I left. Once outside the doors, however, a strong impulse, almost physical, made me turn toward the dollar racks outside. There, bound in red, on the first shelf I consulted, it sat. The second incident, almost identical to the first, involved a twin-volume set of the correspondence of Edward Fitzgerald.

Probably everyone has a secret wish list: one with which reality occasionally intersects. There are other books on mine. I would love, for example, to walk into a bookstore and discover some unknown work by W. G. Sebald; or a volume collecting all the early drafts of Marguerite Yourcenar's *Memoirs of Hadrien*; or a second volume of *Invisible Cities* by Italo Calvino; or, let's really go for it here, a facsimile of Tamsen Donner's journal, the one that was lost. Extravagances aside, I know that somewhere out there (and certainly on a certain shelf in Massachusetts) *Some Chinese Ghosts*, the one that I had hoped for, exists. I just have to put my hands on it again.

Nancy Huston

Address Unknown—Kressmann Taylor

Here is a perfectly astonishing little book—a short story that was lost then found but never actually recognized for what it was. First published in *Story* magazine in 1938, "Address Unknown" was so popular that the *Reader's Digest* rapidly served up a condensed version to their three million American readers. Britain got interested; the story appeared in translation in several European countries. Then, unfortunately, the Second World War broke out and the story was forgotten. At last, fifty years later (1995), it was reissued in hardcover and blithely described by its editor as "the perfect short story"—the irony being that neither the first nor the second publication made any allusion to the fact that the author's intent was to warn people about the imminence of the Holocaust.

Kressmann Taylor was an American, married and the mother of three children, who worked in advertising in the 1920s. Using a number of actually existing letters as her starting point, she invented a stunning piece of short fiction in the form of a correspondence, carried on from 1932 to 1934, between two German men—one Jewish (Eisenstein) and the other a Gentile (Schulse)—friends and partners of an art gallery in San Francisco. Schulse, who is married and a father, recently had an affair with Eisenstein's sister, Griselle, and although he broke it off he still cares deeply for the young woman, now a successful actress in Vienna. Schulse himself has decided to return to Germany with his family, and Eisenstein writes to keep him abreast of the art gallery news.

As the months go by, Schulse, though wary at first, gradually gets caught up in the fervour of the new National Socialist Party in Germany. By 1933, having become a fanatic supporter of Hitler, he asks that Eisenstein cease writing to him completely, as letters from a Jew could be harmful to his image and his position in the municipal government. When Griselle knocks on his door a while later, in hopes of finding refuge and protection from the persecution she's enduring on stage and off, he turns her away, allows her to be captured and shot to death and drily informs Eisenstein of what has happened. From this point on, Eisenstein undertakes to destroy his former friend by sending him a series of jocular, enthusiastic, coded letters containing numerous references to the affection of his Jewish friends and family; the last of these letters is returned to him with the sinister stamp "Address Unknown"—certain proof that Schulse has been interned if not physically eliminated.

Kressmann Taylor was not clairvoyant, she was just exceptionally attentive to and anxious about what was going on in the world. Her style is strikingly economical: thanks to the "letters" device, the main events of the story are suggested rather than stated. It's a pity she was unable to get her message across—but then, no one expects fiction to change the course of history, right?

Siri Hustvedt

I Served the King of England—Bohumil Hrabel

Bohumil Hrabel's *I Served the King of England* is not truly a forgotten book. It has been translated into many languages from its original Czech, was in print in paperback the last time I checked, and yet I have discovered that the name of this writer means nothing to most people, and in this sense, Hrabel must qualify as a writer who has been lost to many.

Ditie, our hero, is a runt—in every sense of the word. He is tiny, not five feet tall, but he is also small of mind and short of social status, and he spends years trying to raise himself to the level of the rest of the world. But little by little, Ditie's life exacts a change in him, and the transformation of Ditie is a beautiful thing to read, because the book is also a parable of the little man in Europe, before, during and after the Second World War.

Ditie starts off as a busboy in the Golden Prague Hotel. Here he learns that delicious food, beautiful women, and what he craves above all—respect—are all available for a price. When a sausage-slicing-machine salesman covers the floor of Ditie's hotel room with crown notes, the busboy's dream of riches takes focus. He moves up in the world, training under a headwaiter with an uncanny ability to predict a guest's nationality, habits, and what he or she is going to order. When questioned about his gnostic gifts, the man replies: "I served the King of England." Ditie's obsessive desire to prove he is equal to his superiors, coupled with his love for a Nazi girl, turns him into a German collaborator during the war, but like the bosses in the hotels where he once worked, the Germans snub him. When the balance of power shifts, Ditie is delighted to find himself mistakenly imprisoned as a communist. Eventually, he buys a hotel of his own, becomes a millionaire, and then loses everything in the paroxysms of Czech society after the war. At the novel's end, he is living in the remote countryside with a horse, a goat and a cat. Every day he repairs roads. Every evening he writes, and at last he is happy.

But it is the energy of the language that makes this book live. Its repetitions work like an urgent incantation on the reader. Its sentences have a Gogolian extension to them, but unlike Gogol, Hrabel does not elaborate an idea through metaphors that become literal, but through associations linked by memory. One event generates another, and Hrabel allows each offshoot its own sublime growth. The boss of the Hotel Tichota is confined to a wheelchair:

> He would be sitting there in his wheelchair and as usual something would be making him uncomfortable, a rumpled blanket that needed smoothing out, so we would fasten a belt around his waist, like fireman have, with a ring on it. This was the same kind the miller Mr. Radimsky's two children used to wear when they played near where the millrace joined the river, and whenever Hary or Vintir—those were their names—toddled toward the millrace, the Saint Bernard would get up, grab the ring in his mouth, and pull Hary and Vintir out of danger. That's exactly what we did with the boss ...

With this contraption, Ditie and a co-worker haul the boss up and out of his chair. As he dangles helplessly above their heads they busy themselves with adjustments for his comfort. The speed of association mimics the leaps of thought, while the images resemble the distortions of dreams.

The suspended boss is only one of many stories within the story, that together reverberate as metaphors for spiritual and political life: the

Rabelaisian feast held for the Emperor of Ethiopia, the brain-damaged boy Ditie fathers with his Nazi wife, a mute who obsessively hammers nails into the floor wherever he is, the wife who picks up her drunken husband as if he were "an empty coat" and "tosses" him into the elevator where he "clatters" to the floor. This is not the stuff of realism, and yet these events are not miraculous either. The laws of nature don't break in the book, they bend.

The Vintage International paperback edition, 1990. Illustration by Catherine Denvir, design by Marc J. Cohen

From the beginning the novel's slapstick carries an undercurrent of brutality. The camels for the Ethiopian feast are slaughtered on the hotel lawn. A lusty fight between rival gypsy gangs leaves behind it quarts of blood, bits of flesh and a severed ear. As the story develops, the violence loses its buoyancy. A porter at the Hotel Tichota tortures and kills the tomcat with whom Ditie's own beloved cat has been dallying. Sadism is human, and given the opportunity, it spreads. When Nazi doctors demand a sperm sample from Ditie to verify that his small Slavic self may be wedded to Aryan purity, he thinks of the slaughter around him and cannot get an erection. Ditie finally releases the required specimen, and The Bureau for the Defense of German Honour and Blood gives him a marriage license.

In this preposterous bureau, the surreal and the real collide, and the madness of history forces us to recognize that collision as truth. Had there been no holocaust, the "examination" would have seemed as improbable as the dangling boss. In the book there is a refrain, and with each repetition, its meaning grows: this is "the story," Ditie writes, "of how the unbelievable came true."

John Irving

The Headmaster's Papers—Richard A. Hawley

The Headmaster's Papers, a novel by Richard A. Hawley, was first published in 1983 by a small, independent publisher in Middlebury, Vermont—Paul S. Eriksson. At the time, the author was himself a headmaster; he was a teacher and the director of the upper school division of the University School, an independent school in Cleveland, Ohio. *The Headmaster's Papers* is an epistolary novel—a form I much admire, chiefly for the difficulty of writing a novel with such a limited structure.

The best writer of fiction in the epistolary form is Alice Munro, and I told Alice once that two things prevented me from trying to write an epistolary novel, which I have long been tempted to do. One is that Alice has already written better in this form than anyone likely will, and two is that Richard A. Hawley wrote *The Headmaster's Papers*, an epistolary novel so heartbreaking that no one is likely to surpass its emotional effect in letter form. I sent a copy of the novel to Alice; she liked it very much. We had a further conversation about epistolary novels, and I told her that I thought Hawley's novel was so moving that he establishes a virtual rule for future epistolary novels: namely, the last letter in the novel has to be a suicide note. Nothing else will do.

The Headmaster's Papers is entirely composed of one man's letters—John Greeve's, the suffering headmaster at an all-boys' private school. His name is well-chosen. In Hawley's journal, before he began the novel, he wrote: "Imagine a good man whose props have fallen away." That is John Greeve—a very good man, whose life has been to guide others but who finds himself, in his middle fifties, rudderless and at sea. His letters are to friends, to the angry parents of boys dismissed from school, to his own son—lost to drugs and wandering in Europe, or (the reader presumes) most likely dead. Also, included among Greeve's "papers" are his public addresses to the boys and faculty of his school, and his heartfelt (occasionally too heartfelt) poems, which he submits to various small magazines.

From his letters, we see how impossibly "good" Greeve's standards are; we also see his own efforts to maintain himself, with dignity and grace, slipping. His wife is dying of cancer. When she dies, Greeve gives up. In his last letter to his lost son, Greeve writes: "We are forever in the stands, kid. Sorry." In his suicide notes, to old friends, he writes: "This is not a tragedy. I am used up." But he's wrong; *The Headmaster's Papers* is a tragedy, a fine one.

I implied earlier that the last letter in Hawley's novel is a suicide note, but this isn't exactly true—the suicide note is next to last. The last letter is a kind of PS to the suicide note, or a different kind of suicide note from the first one—call it suicide note number two. Greeve submits a poem to his school's quarterly magazine. To the editor, he writes: "I know we don't print poems as a rule, but since there will be no Headmaster's Letter, maybe you could work it in."

The poem itself is one of John Greeve's best, the closing lines of which can be read as suicide note number three.

> A bright road opening wide to me
>
> Ghost children chanting something
>
> About verbs
>
> They are cheering in waves

Hymns from voices clear and sad

And gone as bells

Hurrying bells, evening bells

School bells banging me back

To school.

Back in 1983, the novel received a fair amount of well-deserved attention—especially for a first novel, and for a small-press publication. *The Boston Globe* compared Hawley to Louis Auchincloss, and Mr. Auchincloss himself wrote in praise of the novel—as did I: "The headmaster is a character ripe with nobility, and with personal failure and hopelessness," I wrote. "Mr. Hawley has the poise and vision of a writer who can create a whole world." It was successful enough to merit a paperback sale—to Bantam, in '84. And in 1992 Eriksson published a revised paperback edition of the novel, with a foreword and afterword by the author. Both are interesting but unnecessary; the novel works best all by itself. Whatever narrative limitations are imposed on an epistolary novel, *The Headmaster's Papers* demonstrates that a good man's suffering can be felt in his letters as keenly as in any other form of storytelling.

The novel can be ordered from Paul S. Eriksson, Publisher, 208 Battell Building, Middlebury, Vermont 05733 ($14.95 US).

Pico Iyer

The Saddest Pleasure—Moritz Thomsen

It's not a classic, and it wasn't a formative work for me, but in recent times I've found myself increasingly haunted by Moritz Thomsen's *The Saddest Pleasure*, last seen in a scanty edition from Graywolf Press in St. Paul, Minnesota. I'd always believed that a travel book should be a journey into life and self that revived them both and reinvigorated hope; to travel is to learn to live again. But Thomsen's cranky and unassimilable book shocks and unsettles me by telling, in effect, of a journey towards extinction.

White-haired, improvident, just released from a Quito hospital and buried (almost literally) in his copy of *Death in Venice* as the book begins, Thomsen sets off on a tour of South America, at the age of sixty-three, not so much in the spirit of a traveller as of a cornered dog, backing away from a group of children throwing stones at him. He's just been cheated out of his farm along the River of Emeralds in Ecuador (by his ex-partner, Ramon), and he has no home any more in America; so he takes to the road, with nothing but a single blue bag, a thousand dollars he's saved up and the reckless candour of one contemplating last things. He stays in two-dollar-a-night hotels, talks only to waiters and whores, and holds his loneliness to him like a security blanket. The highlight of his trip comes in an interview with a famous writer who won't talk to him.

The Saddest Pleasure, in its opening sentence, introduces us to the *despedida*, or ceremonial farewell beloved of South Americans, with Thomsen bidding adieu to his treacherous partner and a family that's the closest thing to his own. It continues on the more or less classic itinerary of the travel book, into the wastelands of memory and self, as its angry narrator struggles to make his peace with the affluent father and America he left long ago. But its end-point, one always senses, is Samarra. In Belem, Thomsen sees—or dreams he sees—three women dressed in black. He sees them again in Recife, and then again in Natal, and it's easy to suspect that the figures are his guides into the epic underworld.

The aim of every travel book, I'd always thought, is to surrender: to give oneself over to one's surroundings so fully that a part of one (the workaday, habit-bound part) dies, and something more enduring comes to light. But Thomsen's book is shadowed by a much more absolute surrender. He truly seems not to care what happens to him, or where he ends up. He loses his one bag and makes few attempts to retrieve it. He boards a boat on the Amazon—akin to Conrad's Congo, he thinks (akin to the Styx, we think)—and scrupulously alienates his fellow passengers by telling them what he thinks of them. A pretty girl offers him her address in Paris, and he shocks her (and us) by refusing it: he'll never see Paris again, he says.

Like a figure so far from hope that he's living out the final sentences of *The Sheltering Sky*, Thomsen builds up what comes to seem a posthumous memorial. Burning his bridges wherever he can, pronouncing death sentences on missionaries and tourists and all those who would foist their ideas upon the world's poor (in other words, himself when young, as a Peace Corps volunteer), he exerts his last will in completing his final testament. Yet just before the journey ends, he finds a kind of absolution in music (always in music), and when he steps out of the book's concluding sentences, it is in the spirit of one stepping out of the confessional, with a conscience cleansed. Something has been purged in him, one feels, and he steps towards the women dressed in black with a sense that *despedidas* have their purpose. The final irony of *The Saddest Pleasure* is that Thomsen continued to live on till his mid-seventies, and his book came out a dozen years after the ceremonial leave-takings it records.

Gordon Johnston

The Wabeno Feast—Wayland Drew

THE WRITER WAYLAND DREW'S intense interest in the human presence in the lands north of Canada's Great Lakes was like a beacon for some of us back in the early 1970s. Born in 1932, Drew lived, intentionally, as a naturalist and teacher, in small towns north of the metropolis of Toronto, and at a distance from its literary world. Before he died in 1998, he had done all kinds of writing, including radio scripts for the CBC, novelizations of films, and fantasy fiction. But his most enduring work had come early in his career, directly out of his passionate devotion to the wilderness. He expressed that moral passion most forcibly in his first novel, *The Wabeno Feast.*

Back then, in 1973, we still remembered having been boy scouts, and our fathers had been soldiers, and everything should have been fine, even with memories of mushroom clouds and Vietnam, but everything went bad. Back then, we were settling into our careers, into our lives; we were expecting adventures *and* we were expecting the worst. Drew's novel preserves perfectly those earnest conversations we had, strung between idealism and cynicism, and our sense that those conversations mattered.

His novel is about four friends who grew up in a northern mill town, where they all fell in love with the scoutmaster's beautiful wife, and from where they all eventually moved south to go to school and find careers. In the main plot of the novel some kind of environmental disaster has critically disabled Toronto and tests the resources and relations of the now-adult friends: a sardonic lawyer, an anguished business executive, a lunatic activist, and a cold-blooded television director. The businessman, Paul Henry, is the central figure; his father was a "halfway man"; too cautious, he died in the war. Paul's son has been killed by poison gas in an industrial accident. So, to escape, Paul and his wife head north by canoe, past the height of land, to a place where they might survive.

On the canoe trip, Paul Henry takes with him the fictional 1785 journal of a fur trader, a factor for the Northwest Company named Drummond MacKay who faced his own ethical crisis in the wilderness. The pages of his journal are spliced into the novel, pages Paul burns after he has read them aloud to his wife Liv.

In the journal MacKay records his attempts to establish friendly

The House of Anansi edition, 1973

relations with the Ojibwa for the purposes of trade, but does not pretend to explain a culture he does not understand. One evening he observes strange figures on the island opposite, wabenos. He learns from a translator, who admits his limitations, that: "This wabeno is the most powerful of their shamans, but whether his influence be curative or pernicious he knew not, although he thought the latter." The remark is, of course, an ironic commentary on the moral ambiguity of European forms of knowledge, European intercourse. Back in the present, Paul and Liv are headed into the past where Reason confronted Nature; they encounter people from Paul's own past, like an outfitter whose new trophies are abandoned watches and clocks, all telling a different time. But the couple is also headed into a possible future. They are going all the way. It is an erotic view of our engagement with the environment, the whole range of relations: rape, lust, promiscuity, seduction, infidelity, and something like love.

The novel was true for us then in a general way, but also startlingly true for me in a particular way. Like the four friends from Sable Creek, I had grown up in northern Ontario, had come south to go to school, and was making the usual compromises required in adult life. While making a living in a prosperous world of commerce and industry, carrying my classical education along with me, I was nostalgic for the north. I'd made the pilgrimage to Agawa to see the painted rocks; I was even writing a book in which the ancient world, the historical Canadian north and the present collided, and had called it *Inscription Rock*.

In the flurry of great Canadian fictions from the early 1970s in which we non-Natives finally turned back to encounter and imagine the first peoples and our failures (I am thinking of Margaret Atwood's *Surfacing*, Rudy Wiebe's *Temptations of Big Bear* and Margaret Laurence's *Diviners*), *The Wabeno Feast* was overshadowed, but it deserves to be read. Today it reads like a dream, a little separate from our lives but as clear as yesterday. But more than a dream, its diagnosis is as acute today as it was then. We see the disease now through a technological scrim of political correctness, a global web of development and protest, of markets and resources. But we recognize the environmental warriors, the leaks, the spills and the television cameras. The moral questions are still the pressing ones. Drew's novel has the simplified outlines and the symmetrical plotting of parables and persistent memories and American movies, but it also has their kinds of elemental force. "News that stays news," Ezra Pound said once of poetry; here in *The Wabeno Feast* perhaps what we find is prophecy that stays prophecy.

Wayne Johnston

A History of Newfoundland
—D. W. Prowse
The Newfoundland Journal of Aaron Thomas, 1794
—Aaron Thomas

NEWFOUNDLAND LITERATURE IS A literature of lost classics. It is the rule for books about Newfoundland to be hard to find or even out of print. There are many reasons for this fact. In the nineteenth century, St. John's was twice destroyed by fire and the only existing copies of many books were lost. Also, Newfoundland books were not highly regarded by that small portion of society that could afford to buy them or knew how to read. Their authors were looked upon as pretentious and provincial, apeing real writers whose most important credential was that they lived elsewhere.

In this, Newfoundland was not unlike many of the colonies. But there is a special way that Newfoundland books are "lost" that has to do with Newfoundland's confederation with Canada in 1949. A book can be in print and easy to find and still be "lost" if no one reads it. And so it is with most of those few Newfoundland books written before 1949 that still exist and, with a modicum of effort, can be found.

There is a misconception, by some people much encouraged, by others simply allowed to go unchallenged, that Newfoundland was "born" in 1949, that in 1949, Canadian history retroactively became our history, that, for instance, "our" first prime minister was Sir John A. MacDonald. The same misconception is applied to pre-confederate Canadian literature. Our actual history and literature now exist in a kind of limbo where not even many archivists set foot.

Given the virtual extinction of Newfoundland's literary past, it is almost impossible to focus on one lost book without giving the impression that for a Newfoundland book to be "lost" is exceptional. I have decided to halve that risk by writing about two very different lost classics of Newfoundland.

Judge D. W. Prowse pointed out in his *A History of Newfoundland*, published by Macmillan in London and New York in 1895, that all that remained of many Newfoundland books were allusions made to them in other books: their author's names, their titles, a paraphrased sentence here and there or, rarely, a single, precious direct quotation. He wrote that the six histories of Newfoundland that preceded his were in large part based on such sources and mostly written by clergymen—and he implied that their purpose was not so much to record history as to reconcile Newfoundlanders to the terms of their existence. In these histories, Prowse complained, dead authors whose books have vanished from the earth were cited as unimpeachable authorities on all sorts of subjects.

He decided that in writing his own book, he would have to begin from scratch. Everything in it is based, as the title page declares, on materials found in the "English, Colonial and Foreign Records." One nearly forgotten Newfoundland writer, Margaret Duley, referred to Prowse's book as "our great history." It remains so to this day, even though most Newfoundlanders, even Newfoundland writers, have never read it. It has been kept in print by the Canadiana Reprint Series. My copy was published by Mika Studio in Belleville, Ontario in 1972. As there were no copies to be found in St. John's, I ordered mine from a rare book dealer in Halifax who found it by computer in a bookshop in New York.

Reading Prowse, one gets the sense that he is trying constantly not to dwell on the likelihood that his book will not be read, or, if read, not

A

HISTORY OF NEWFOUNDLAND

FROM THE

English, Colonial, and Foreign Records

BY

D. W. PROWSE, Q.C.

Judge of the Central District Court of Newfoundland

WITH A PREFATORY NOTE BY EDMUND GOSSE

WITH THIRTY-FOUR COLLOTYPES, OVER THREE HUNDRED TEXT ILLUSTRATIONS, AND NUMEROUS MAPS

London

MACMILLAN AND CO.

AND NEW YORK

1895

Title page from the MacMillan and Co. facsimile edition, 1972

received with the gravity that it deserves. His is the double burden of the historian of a small country. He must not only write well, he must convince the reader that his subject is worthwhile.

But, reading Prowse, one also gets the sense that he believes himself to be heroically engaged, that he is restoring, even salvaging, the past, that he knows that if he doesn't do it, no one will. As if the sheer size of the book itself (eight hundred pages, along with countless maps, charts, tables, etc.) is not proof enough of what it cost him to write it, he says in his introduction, "The labour was so enormous that I have several times dropped it in despair." He seems to have had the sort of ego that begged to be deflated. As a judge, he granted parole to any poacher who agreed to be his guide on hunting trips. He once debated, by way of an exchange of letters in the *Royal Gazette*, the question of his grandfather's true identity. "I am reduced," he told a friend, "to public argument with a total stranger who claims to know better than me who I am descended from." Of his grandfather, the *Encyclopedia of Newfoundland* says laconically: "Born Devon. Married a Mudge."

Because Newfoundland's past is set down nowhere else but in Prowse's book, it is tempting to think that that past begins with him, tempting to think of him as having made it up. And so I often picture him at his desk day after day, year after year, scrupulously, exhaustively, painstakingly inventing Newfoundland. The story of the near-consignment of another Newfoundland book to oblivion can be taken as a measure of how many books there must have been that did not survive.

Aaron Thomas was an able seaman on the HMS *Boston* in 1794 when Britain was at war with France. The Boston, which convoyed trading ships from England to Newfoundland, made it safely to St. John's. Thomas wrote an account of the seven months he spent in and around the city in the form of a letter to a friend that was never sent. He gave a rare view of life below decks on a British naval ship and an even rarer view of life in what he called “the grog shops of St. John’s.”

The *Boston* put in at many ports along the Southern Shore. Thomas seems to have had what amounts to “widow radar,” finding a widow eager to cook for him every place he went. In Ferryland alone, he found two. There is a Mrs. Keene who “is left in good circumstances, having fourteen cows, which in Newfoundland puts the proprietor on a par with Job in point of riches.” There is a Mrs. Tree, widow of Captain Tree, “an American Loyalist who lost considerable property when the British troops abandoned Boston.” Mrs. Tree, Thomas writes to his friend, has now had to resort to “keeping a house of entertainment called the London Inn … where not even an Epicure could find fault with a single dish.” He commiserates with a woman who, having grown accustomed to the “Bon Ton” in London, came out to Newfoundland when her husband died and is now married to a man with whom, in her former life, she would not have deigned to speak—“a cod hauler.”

Thomas wrote to his friend: “Do you know that, as I write these sheets, I fancy I am telling a tale? I sitting on one side and you on the other?”

These are among my favourite lines in all of literature. It is no longer possible for writers to write as unselfconsciously as that, to get halfway through telling a story before they even begin to suspect that they are telling one. His is the innocent amazement of a man who, in mid-composition, discovers he is writing and at the same time has no expectation of ever being read by anyone except his "friend."

After the *Boston* left St. John's, Aaron Thomas, following a series of misadventures, died of scurvy in the West Indies. More than eighty years later, the leather-bound manuscript of his letter to his friend was found and bought by a Newfoundlander at a used bookshop in England. After passing through many hands over the course of nearly a hundred years, it was published simultaneously by Longmans of London and Longmans Canada in 1968 under the title *The Newfoundland Journal of Aaron Thomas, 1794*. It has long since gone out of print and copies of it are all but impossible to find. I first read it in the rare books section at the National Library in Ottawa in 1981.

There is more life in Aaron Thomas's letter to his friend than there is in the combined correspondence of all the English governors of Newfoundland. It is as true that Newfoundland literature begins with Thomas as it is that Newfoundland history begins with Prowse.

Janice Kulyk Keefer

The Primer

Well and truly lost—this book I came across in childhood and kept for my own. A Russian primer, circa 1923, printed on stock so grainy it owed more to pumice than paper. Illustrations of earnest Russian schoolchildren—the girls with strictly braided hair and lavish bows—done in blurry ink that seemed to dissolve as I looked at them. The Byzantine elegance of those Cyrillic letters I loved like secrets, coded treasures, my tongue the key.

Vanished. It used to live in my study, not far from where my other Russian keepsake lies—a narrow brass pen tray, stamped with the Tsar's eagle and the date 1917. The kind of nibbed straight pen this tray deserves isn't made any more: the tray lies empty, flaunting its imperial impress in the face of a primer bearing an equal and opposite stamp. For though no Lenin in cloth cap and natty, spade-shaped beard strode through its pages, the very harshness of the paper and crudeness of the ink might have been singing the "Internationale" for a whole nation of soon-to-be-literate children.

For all I know, Marina Tsvetayeva's daughter, the one who perished of starvation in a Moscow orphanage, might have learned to read from the pages of this primer, white ribbons like fat white ghosts pinching the ends of her braids. And that elderly, Russian-born woman I met by chance in Highgate so many years ago may have used this very book when she taught a schoolroom of peasant children in Sverdlosk, children so poor they came to school on alternate days, sharing the one pair of boots each family had between them. That schoolteacher went her own circuitous route from Tsarist to Soviet Russia and then, somehow, South Africa, to end up in a salubrious English suburb. But how did that primer come to be in Toronto, how did it make its way to my parents' house, where books arrived like distinguished foreign visitors to be politely, anxiously put up? And where in the world is it now, this very moment, when I reach out for it?

A slender volume with cloth-covered boards—sober, grey cloth, factory-issue. An act of, an ode to, disintegration just to turn its ashy pages. Perhaps it hasn't been borrowed from its shelf and never returned—

perhaps it hasn't—as I begin to fear—been thrown out in a fit of cleaning. Perhaps it hasn't fallen behind the bookshelf-far-too-heavy-to-move, that limbo of printed matter, that forlorn lost-and-never-found. Perhaps it has slowly disappeared *in situ* over the years it's been in my possession, turning phantom. But leaving what behind?

The ghost of two illustrations and two words. This is what I remember most clearly of the contents—two facing pages, on which appeared two pictures of the same boy, sitting at the same desk, with the same white cat who has jumped up to investigate whether fish might be swimming in the inkpot. The text is a two-word morality play. For in the first illustration—a mere line drawing—the boy is taking his straight pen and darting drops of blackest ink on the perfect blankness of the cat's back. Cyrillic letters strut below: XA! XA! XA! The "X" is pronounced like the "ch" in the Scottish word "loch," if you let yourself go to town, gutturally, with that "ch." It is the very trumpet-call of Schadenfreude, that perverse joy discovered in the misery of others. What enchanted me about this illustration was its mate, on the facing page—a picture of the same cat knocking over the inkpot on the same boy's copybook, making a beautiful black pool and provoking bitter lamentation, expressed by the reverse of those Cyrillic letters that appeared before: AX! AX! AX! Pronounced like the German "ach," but with far more phlegm.

I must have known, even as a child, that justice didn't work as concisely as this. I've learned, on growing up, that life is made out of complications, just as paper's made out of a stew of pulp and rags. But I've kept the impress of these illustrations long after the book that sheltered them has vanished—I even begin to believe that my Russian primer has done its disappearing trick by distilling itself into those two words of text, exultation, grief and a whole world of puzzles and astonishments between.

Wendy Lesser

The Old Wives' Tale—Arnold Bennett

I HAVE AN EXPERIMENT for you to try. The next time you're at a literary gathering, ask ten people whether they've ever read Arnold Bennett. Now, by "literary gathering," I do not mean your run-of-the-mill publisher's cocktail party. For the experiment to work, you have to choose a group consisting of people who actually *read.*

Even in such a select group, I predict, no more than one in ten will have read an Arnold Bennett novel. But fully half your sample is likely to pipe up with the information that though they haven't read Bennett himself, they *have* read Virginia Woolf's essay "Mr. Bennett and Mrs. Brown." And that essay, they will suggest, made it abundantly clear that there was no need ever to read Arnold Bennett.

I find it disturbing that Virginia Woolf, the possessor of an intense but extremely limited form of genius, should have been able, in the course of just sixty or seventy years, to crowd a great novelist like Arnold Bennett right off the literary map. It is as if you had planted a delightfully unusual groundcover in your garden, only to discover some years later that its rampant spread has killed your favourite oak. (Well, not oak, exactly. Charles Dickens is an oak. Bennett is more like an unruly old apple tree: he could use some pruning, but the fruit is delicious.)

Woolf's objection to Bennett is that he fails to create what she considers real characters, and she singles out some passages from his novel *Hilda Lessways* to prove it. I'll admit that *Hilda Lessways* is full of flaws; like many great novelists, Bennett wrote a number of mediocre books. But he did produce one indisputable masterpiece, *The Old Wives' Tale*, and that is where I recommend you start. Each time I'm in the midst of reading it, I think it the best novel ever written. Near the beginning, it has a scene viewed from a tiny baby's perspective; towards the middle, it describes a woman's reaction to a public guillotining; it ends, naturally, with a funeral. In between it has everything from the details of a small-town draper's store to the inflationary economy of Paris during the Franco–Prussian war. It follows the lives of two sisters—Constance, who stays home in the provincial "Five Towns" and prosaically marries, and Sophia, who runs off with a handsome cad—and comes down on neither side. Its virtues are its generosity, its breadth and its felt evocation of a tangible reality.

Bennett writes marvellously on the stuff of life. In his best novels (which include *Clayhanger* and *Riceyman Steps* as well as *The Old Wives' Tale*), he makes you understand what it must have been like to sit at a Victorian deathbed, to give in to an autocratic father or a miserly husband, to work as a servant or a printer, and to live out one's life in a smoky little industrial town or an obscure corner of London, all the while longing for a cleaner, larger, more satisfying existence.

There have only been a few modern novelists who possessed this nineteenth-century ability to convey a sense of time and place. Christopher Isherwood was one of them, which is why Thom Gunn, praising Isherwood's novels, was able to say: "It is surely of permanent interest that reading them we may imagine what it was like to live in the Berlin of the 1930s or the Los Angeles of the 1960s." But Virginia Woolf did not believe in such a thing as "permanent interest." She believed, as she said in her Bennett essay, that "on or about December 1910, human character changed," which meant that all novels written prior to that date were obsolete. The very idea of accurately conveying a historical period would have seemed to her ludicrous, misguided; the only focus she valued was inward. And her view is the one that seems to have prevailed.

It is unfair of me to blame the whole catastrophe on Virginia Woolf. She had history on her side. Late-twentieth-century history wanted *To the Lighthouse* rather than *The Old Wives' Tale*. It wanted fleeting impressionistic glances, fragmented cubist narratives and highly crafted, self-consciously poetic, self-advertisingly sensitive lines of prose. It wanted thin novels rather than fat ones; it didn't want to have to get through a lot of excess information about anyone or anything. It wanted, above all, a guarantee that it was getting someone's exclusive personal vision: the inside story, the secret life exposed, the piercingly revelatory moment. But in exchange for this, we gave up something—call it freedom, or largeness, or whatever it is that Arnold Bennett, at his best, so movingly possesses.

Philip Levine

Ha! Ha! Among the Trumpets—Alun Lewis

Once a month on Thursday afternoons in the late forties the poets of Detroit—or at least those I knew—would gather in the Miles Poetry Room on the second floor of the Wayne University Library, housed in Old Main, the run-down, stately mansion which originally housed the entire college and was located at the corner of Cass and Warren, a busy pathway to both the downtown, then still lively, and the great factories to the west. The room was named after Theodore Miles, a young English teacher turned naval officer who had died in action in the Pacific and willed his extensive modern poetry collection to the university. The dozen of us ranging in age from our teens to early fifties came together to encourage our differing efforts, and at each meeting discuss poetry, "real poetry" or our own. At each meeting one of us presented a reading and discussion of a particular poet who had fired our imagination: earlier in the fall of '49 Paul Petrie had done Elinor Wylie; Bernard Strempek had done Hart Crane;

Florence Goodman, Muriel Rukeyser; Bill Leach, George Barker; in the spring, Richard Werry—the only faculty member in our group—would do Dylan Thomas, and Bob Huff would do Robert Lowell. On a particular gloomy Thursday in early November, I had just finished a nervous and I hoped eloquent presentation of Wilfred Owen, then my favourite poet, when Bernie Strempek rose from one of the threadbare sofas and selected a forgotten anthology from one of the lower shelves that housed the collection and, still standing, read the assembled group in his faltering tenor voice of great delicacy and precision a poem I had never heard before, "In Hospital: Poona." As the late afternoon grey light filtered through the high windows of the corner room I could see Bernie's eyes brim with tears as they always did when he read or recited poetry not his own. ("He has the face of a fallen angel," a friend would later say.)

After the reading there was a long minute of silence after which I asked, "Who wrote that?" Bernie explained that it was Alun Lewis, a young Welsh officer who had died in Burma late in the recent war. In the poem the speaker describes his efforts not to fall asleep but to lay awake to reach imaginatively his beloved, back in Wales furled "in the same dark watch as I." In imagination he sees that whole world left behind, his world, "the great mountains, Daydd and Llewelyn, / Plynlimmon, Cader Idris, and Eryri / Threshing the darkness" and also "the small nameless mining valley" which had been home. It struck me almost as a version of MacLeish's great poem "You Andrew Marvell" suddenly given a more human and vulnerable face.

After the meeting broke up and before I joined my fellow poets at a nearby lounge for a post-meeting bull session, I found—much to my surprise, in the stacks of the regular library—two small, black cardboard-bound copies of Alun Lewis's second and posthumous collection of poetry, *Ha! Ha! Among the Trumpets*, published in England in a cheap wartime edition in '45 and acquired by our library in '47. Neither had ever been checked out. One of them, I'm moderately ashamed to admit, has never been checked out, for it's with me still.

The book contains a short, brilliant introduction by Robert Graves, who along with the poet's wife, helped edit it. Graves includes a letter from Lewis in response to several suggestions he'd made. The letter reached Graves a day or two before the poet's death. Lewis had written: "I've taken a sardonic title for the poems from Job 39, 'Ha! Ha! Among the Trumpets.' You know the beautiful chapter. The liberty of the wild ass, the lovelessness of the ostrich, the intrepidity of the horse. These are the particulars. The infinite, of which I can never be sure, is God the Maker. I prefer the ostrich's eggs warming in the sun." Graves concludes the introduction with fragments of a letter written by Lewis from Burma to his wife Gweno. They close as follows: "… I find myself quite unable to express at once the passion of Love, the coldness of Death (Death is cold), and the fire that beats against resignation, 'acceptance.' Acceptance seems so spiritless, protest so vain. In between the two I live."

Ha! Ha! Among the Trumpets contains the single most beautiful poem I know of to rise out of the nightmare of that war. "Song (On seeing dead bodies floating off the Cape)" is spoken by a woman who has intuited the death of her soldier-lover at sea. It ends:

> The flying fish like kingfishers
> Skim the sea's bewildered crests,
> The whales blow steaming fountains,
> The seagulls have no nests
> Where my lover sways and rests.

We never thought to buy and sell
This life that blooms or withers in the leaf,
And I'll not stir, so he sleeps well,
Though cell by cell the coral reef
Builds an eternity of grief.

But oh the drag and dullness of my Self;
The turning seasons wither in my head,
All this slowness, all this hardness,
The nearness that is waiting in my bed,
The gradual self-effacement of the dead.

ALAN LIGHTMAN

Far Away and Long Ago—W. H. Hudson

A NUMBER OF YEARS AGO, before the days of amazon.com, I journeyed cross-country to Powell's bookstore in Portland, Oregon in a last attempt to find a certain long-out-of-print book by W. H. Hudson. I was already a great admirer of Hudson's more famous *Green Mansions*, a terribly sad novel about a romance in the green forests of South America that had haunted me for years. After wandering through acres and acres of used books at Powell's, I entered a small clearing and spotted the relevant shelf. And there, I found five copies of the object of my desire. Out of good sportsmanship, I bought only three. The book was Hudson's *Far Away and Long Ago*, a memoir of the author's childhood in the pampas of Argentina. "Far away," because Hudson lived most of the rest of his life in England. "Long ago," because he did not begin writing this book about his youth in mid-nineteenth-century Argentina until sixty years later, in 1915, at the age of seventy-four. Then, while laid up for six weeks recovering from a serious illness, Hudson's childhood in the Buenos Aires region came back to him in a startling avalanche of detail, sights and sounds and smells, strange visitors, a farming life with his immigrant parents and six brothers and sisters in a beautiful but wild country cut off from their roots, an oasis of civilization like Karen Blixen's home in Kenya.

Far Away and Long Ago is a mysterious voyage to another place and time. But it is also artful storytelling, a poignant collection of tales about the odd and wonderfully painted characters who made occasional stops at the Hudson family house on their travels through the lawless countryside. The huge Captain Scott, "with a great round face of a purplish colour, like the sun setting in glory," or the itinerant tutor Mr. Trigg, "a short, stoutish, almost fat little man, with grey hair, clean-shaved sunburnt face, a crooked nose which had been broken or was born so, clever mobile mouth, and blue-grey eyes with a humorous twinkle in them and crow's feet at the corners." Mr. Trigg was not liked by his young charges, for "he was a schoolmaster who hated and despised teaching as much as children in the wild hated to be taught."

What is most magical to me about this book is its exquisite description of landscape. Hudson wrote extensively on naturalist subjects, especially ornithology, and his portraits are so fresh and achingly beautiful that I can recite some of them by heart, as I do favourite lines from the sonnets of Shakespeare. Here, for example, is Hudson's description of a flock of field finches, roosting in one of his beloved peach trees:

> The field finch does not twitter or chirp and has no break or sudden change in its song, which is composed of a series of long-drawn notes, the first somewhat throaty but growing clearer and brighter towards the end, so that when thousands sing together it is as if they sang in perfect unison, the effect on the hearing being like that on the sight of flowing water or of rain when the multitudinous falling drops appear as silvery grey lines on the vision.

I cannot read such passages, or recite them to myself, without seeing in my mind the old man lying in a bed somewhere in the south of England. I can almost hear his breathing. And then, lying there, near the end of his life, he re-experiences his childhood far away and long ago, vividly re-creates it, re-creates a world, I sense, larger and more true than it ever was. I want my field finches like Hudson described them. I want his peach trees and winter violet, his black acacias and lombardy poplars. Which world is real? The world I love more is the world in memory, in words.

Derek Lundy

The Cruise of the Cachalot and *The Log of a Sea-Waif* —Frank T. Bullen

EACH TIME I HAD to fight some other boy in the schoolyard because of my funny accent, I thought of Frank T. Bullen.

My family emigrated to Canada when I was eleven, and we settled in a small farming village in Ontario that hadn't seen an immigrant in three generations. My English accent triggered brawls several times a week until even my *laissez-faire* Irish father became fed up with my bloody noses and torn clothes. He complained to the principal who called the police, and we junior sluggers had to promise the local copper, a hulking drunkard who lived in the apartment downstairs to ours, not to fight any more.

The end of hostilities was a great relief for me; I was battle-weary and not particularly courageous. I had fought out of desperation and fear of the worse things that would happen if I didn't. And I'm sure I could not have withstood it all without Frank Bullen's example.

Frontispiece from the Hearst & Company edition, 1898

Bullen was an English sailor who spent a good part of his life before the mast and on the quarterdecks of square-rigged sailing ships all around the world in the late nineteenth century. He described himself as a London "street Arab" before he ran away to sea at the age of twelve. In *The Log of a Sea-Waif*, the story of his first four years on board ship, he describes his induction into the harsh clamour of the fo'c's'le. He had to learn the strict routines and precise skills of a square-rigger seaman while struggling to establish a newcomer's place in the hierarchy of the older and stronger crew.

A veteran seaman at eighteen, Bullen, like Ishmael, shipped out on a New Bedford whaler. The vessel followed the usual meandering years-long trajectory of wind-borne whaling ships, its crew hunting bowheads, humpbacks and the long-jawed, oil-rich sperm whales close-to with harpoon and lance. Bullen's account of the voyage, a non-fiction *Moby Dick*, was published in 1897 as *The Cruise of the Cachalot*. Bullen worked his way up on merit, not privilege—climbing "over the bowsprit" and not "through the cabin window"—to become a first mate. Eventually he came ashore for good and, like Conrad, he wrote books: these memoirs and more than thirty nautical adventure novels.

When we left for Canada, my father's best friend gave me a volume of Bullen's two memoirs as an emigration present. It must have been an expensive book, especially by the standards of the straitened England of the time. Bound in soft navy-blue leather with pen-and-ink line drawings, it was by far the finest of the handful of books I owned.

LETTER received by the Author from Mr. RUDYARD KIPLING, as the book was passing through the Press.

DEAR MR. BULLEN,—It is immense—there is no other word. I've never read anything that equals it in its deep-sea wonder and mystery; nor do I think that any book before has so completely covered the whole business of whale-fishing, and at the same time given such real and new sea-pictures. You have thrown away material enough to make five books, and I congratulate you most heartily. It's a new world that you've opened the door to.

Very sincerely,

RUDYARD KIPLING.

ROTTINGDEAN, *Nov.* 22, 1898.

Letter received by the author from Kipling in time for publication

It was also the best quality work I possessed; in my almost bookless family, my library then was a few Biggles and Red Ryder potboilers and Beano comics. In my edition, I remember a foreword by Rudyard Kipling. He praised Bullen's storytelling and wrote that the sailor's adventurous life was the material for a hundred tales. Bullen's plain, modest narratives were, nevertheless, stirring and vigorous evocations of the great, expansive world of the sea. They abruptly opened up to me, a descendant of generations of naval ratings and merchant seamen, the realization that I too would go to sea one day; Bullen jogged my genes.

His book is long gone now, unaccountably missing in one of my family's moves. If my recollection of his accounts—both are out of print—are therefore vague and incomplete, their effect on me when I read them was vivid and enduring. Instead of being condemned to the petty and ignoble order of school and its discontents, a boy my age had found himself on the decks and in the yardarms of a full-rigged sailing ship bound, it seemed to me, for limitless adventure. During my schoolyard pummelling, I thought: If Frank Bullen could do that, I should certainly be able to fight off a few bullies before I go home to family, a hot supper and a soft bed.

David Malouf

The Life of Rossini—Stendhal

There are moments when, by the rarest good fortune, two great spirits come into conjunction so that we get the perfect distillation of the one through the mind of the other. So it is with Stendhal's life of Rossini.

Rossini is surely the most natural genius who ever lived. Music bubbled out of him as from a spring. The Italian language finds in him a musical expression so immediate, so essential to its genius, that it is as if, like one of his zanier characters, he had hit upon a mechanical device for turning the elements of speech into instant melody. His invention, his wit, his lightness, his fascination for every sort of quirk—we recognize his own in the obsessive recurrence of the rolling crescendo in which he and his characters find themselves helplessly caught up as in a demonic machine—are in the real sense of the word superficial, of the surface, but it is superficiality raised to the level of the purest spirit. And who better to appreciate this than his great contemporary for whom *esprit* and all that is spiritual constitute the very essence of life energy and joy in being.

Stendhal knows that it is Mozart who is the supreme master. Pensive, melancholy, Mozart's music deals with real emotion, and that of the highest; Rossini knows nothing of these. "The science of harmony," Stendhal writes, "may make whatever progress it pleases, still it will be seen, with astonishment, that all that can be done has already been anticipated in Mozart." But Mozart is German, Rossini the apotheosis of all things Mediterranean. These national variations fascinate Stendhal, but in the end he too is a Mediterranean. He is the analyst *par excellence*, the psychologiser, the acute discriminator; most of all, the worshipper at the shrine of sheer invention. He also has some great stories to tell.

Of the Milanese nobleman, for example, who in 1809, to prove that Mozart could both be played and enjoyed, even by Italians, even if the musicians (a thing unheard of in Italy) had to "start together and come out at the last note exactly at the same moment," gathered together a group of the best symphonists in the town and half a dozen singers, and, "with all the profound secrecy of a conspiracy," shut them up in the various apartments of his palace till they had mastered (it took them six months) the "principle concerted pieces and finales of *Don Giovanni*"—then let them loose on the local dilettanti.

Then there are his nights at the theatre. Like the occasion at Como in 1814 when he heard Rossini's first opera *Demetrio e Polibio*. It was very much a family affair, sung by two sisters and their father, the Mombelli. "The Quartet," Stendhal writes,

> was not only encored but, according to an ancient custom at Como, was called for a third time, when a friend of the family came forward and declared that the ladies had lately been much indisposed, and if the encore of this quartetto was insisted upon, it would perhaps disable them from doing justice to the remainder of the opera. "But is there any other piece so strong?" "Certainly," replied the gentleman, "a duet and two or three other pieces." This assurance had the desired effect, and the enthusiasm of the parterre of Como was for the moment pacified.

(A good editor at this point, like Nicholas N. Coe, will tell us that

Demetrio e Polibio was not given at Como in 1814, and that in that year Stendhal was not in Italy.)

This is not a book for purists. Stendhal's inventions are almost as outrageous as Rossini's and have the same love of the ridiculous, the same assurance and brio, the same unconcern too for the limiting conditions of mere truth. What they are true to is his sense of style, his passion for music, his response to the boundless energy of Rossini's art, which conquers a whole continent as rapidly and as brilliantly as that other force of nature, Bonaparte; but these triumphs, light as they are, all movement and air, are destined to last.

Harry Mathews

On Growth and Form—D'Arcy Wentworth Thompson

(The Pursuit of the Whole—on D'Arcy Wentworth Thompson)

1

UNCERTAINTY SHROUDS THE BEGINNING. Let us say that it occurred in 1944—a reasonable probability—when my father was overseas and my mother rented a summer cottage for the two of us in Wainscott, Long Island. I was fourteen at the time. One evening my mother and I were invited for dinner at Mary Callery's house on the North Shore, or perhaps on Peconic Bay. The time and place do not matter all that much. Mary Callery was my mother's closest friend, beautiful, smart, temperamental, much involved with the international art community, herself a sculptor. There were other guests: the architects Philip Johnson and Mies van der Rohe, newly arrived in America.

Mary Callery, Philip Johnson, and my mother drank dry martinis—

no doubt more than two. I probably drank Coke; I don't know what Mies drank, but I do know that after a while the martini drinkers entered a gay and gossipy realm where Mies and I had no part. Towards the end of the meal I went and sat next to him. I had been told he was a great architect. The prospect of talking to him was interesting because my father was also an architect, serious if not great. So I did not hesitate to question Mies about his work. We talked for about an hour. I suppose that having a fourteen-year-old as listener was better than no company at all; at any rate, he spoke to me seriously and without condescension. I have forgotten everything he said except for one thing: he insisted that all his notions of architectural space had been drawn from a book called *On Growth and Form*, the work of someone called D'Arcy Wentworth Thompson. (When I later mentioned book and author to various literary mentors, none had ever heard of them.)

2

During my late adolescence I was a book stealer. I loved books, not just to read but to own, and there was no way I could buy all I wanted. Because I stole for love, I stole self-righteously. It took time for me to realize that if Scribner's could afford my pilfering, I was doing palpable damage to places like the Holliday Bookshop. At the age of eighteen I stopped altogether.

In 1952 I moved to France with my wife and daughter. In Paris we became close friends with Tony and Eve Bonner. Two years later, the four of us decided to try living in Majorca, reputedly pleasant and unquestionably cheap. Tony was as much a bookworm as I. Faced with an indeterminate stay on a then out-of-the-way island, we took a brief trip to London to stock up on useful books. We spent most of our daylight hours in Foyle's, viewing and reviewing its innumerable shelves.

It was during our first morning in that bookstore that I at last saw a copy of *On Growth and Form* (Cambridge University Press, revised edition, 2 vols.). It was late afternoon of the following day when I mustered the courage to steal it. I was by then in a pitiful state. I hadn't stolen a book in years; my earlier recklessness had deserted me (I was now a husband and father). Even in pluckier days I would have hesitated before smuggling two fat volumes out of a store milling with attentive salesmen. But the unforeseen resurgence of a title pronounced once ten years earlier had set me trembling with superstitious lust. (I could not begin to contemplate paying the twenty pounds it cost—almost two hundred pounds in today's money).

I spent an inwardly frantic, outwardly reasonable hour executing my theft, moving the two volumes separately and in stages from the middle of the second floor towards the ground-floor exit, camouflaging the manoeuvre by bringing books I planned to buy to the cashier nearest my point of escape. At last *On Growth and Form* was settled, not too conspicuously, on a rack between my cashier and the nearby door. I paid for my other books—over a dozen, as I remember—and on my way out picked up my covert objects of desire and walked out into Charing Cross Road. I did not look back. I did not run. I blessed the pedestrian throng.

3

That autumn *On Growth and Form* followed me to Majorca; back to Paris two years later; finally, two years after that, to Lans-en-Vercors (a mountain village near Grenoble). I wrote and published a novel. My marriage ended. I published more novels. My children went away. For a while I lived in Venice, without my books. I returned to Lans to begin life with a new family. I began teaching in America. My father died, my best friend died, my mother died. We moved to Paris. In 1996 we began spending summers in Lans once again; and it was there, on July 29, 1997, that I began reading my last stolen book. My progress was interrupted between September 23 and February 11, 1998. On July 18, once again in Lans, I finished *On Growth and Form*.

Near the end of his work, D'Arcy Thompson writes:

> The biologist, as well as the philosopher, learns to recognise that the whole is not merely the sum of its parts. It is this, and much more than this. For it is not a bundle of parts but an organisation of parts, of parts in their mutual arrangement, fitting one with another, in what Aristotle calls a "single and individual principle of unity"; and this is no merely metaphysical conception, but is in biology the fundamental truth which lies at the basis of Geoffroy's (or Goethe's) law of "compensation" or "balancement of growth."

W. S. Merwin

The Gate of Horn—G. R. Levy

I AM NOT SURE to what degree G. R. (Rachel) Levy's *The Gate of Horn* is "lost." It is a book which has haunted me for more than half my life, a kind of key that seems to have made its way to me like some benign animal in a fairy tale. There are aspects of her book which probably influenced my sense of what it means to be human; once read they were never quite forgotten. That is true, in some way, of the whole thrust of her story.

G. R. Levy was an English archaeologist, much of whose field work was done in the 1930s in Iraq. She became increasingly drawn to the evolution of the myth of the labyrinth and its relation to the development of beliefs about the underworld, resurrection and the afterlife. Her researches led her to the Megalithic sites of Malta and southern Brittany, then to the Paleolithic sites of southwest France and the Pyrenees, and eventually to studies of Megalithic sites in southern Asia, the Pacific and the Americas. I have no idea what place her work may have in the world of academic archaeology at present, but the course of her argument, its range and erudition and luminous brilliance, made the book a treasure as I read it, years ago, in London. It struck me somewhat as *The Golden Bough* had done, but its argument seemed even more immediate and pertinent, closer to the coherence of a work of art.

Rachel Levy was also a classicist, and part of her story is concerned with the development—as seen through burial practices, symbols, and maps of return—of the concept of the individual soul, the person or aspect of a person that might be reborn, that suffered and hoped and was remembered in myths. Her pursuit leads from the end of the Ice Age to the poetry of ancient Greece. To Homer, "and the hero's naked challenge to Fate ..." and "the expression in art of the Herakleitean definition": a man's character is his destiny. What we know of the people who stood before the symbols of the labyrinth at the tomb doors at the end of the Ice Age is their dread of death, their bafflement and desperate hope in the face of it, their need to believe in something still unidentified in themselves. This book traces that gradually crystallizing sense of the self. "Each hero, as he emerges, brings with him a past world, for recreation by a divinity whose nature has been recast by their mutual struggle. By this time the other characters have fallen away. The whole previous action takes places as an imaginative experience. Orestes and Oedipus face the Gods alone."

It is a book of daring and great learning, from a generation of great learning and great breakthroughs. Jung, Cornford, Sir Arthur Evans, H. Schliemann seem to hover around her era and her theme. *The Gate of Horn* certainly seems like a classic to me, and yet for years now—for what may be a generation—I have seldom mentioned it to anyone who seemed to have heard of it. It was published by Faber & Faber in 1948. Whether there was ever an American edition I do not know. Perhaps a classic is a work that one imagines should be common knowledge, but more and more often isn't.

ANCHEE MIN

I Want to Go to School—Yu-pao Gao

THE BOOK WAS CALLED *I Want to Go to School* by Yu-pao Gao published by The People's Publishing House of China. I was eleven years old when I got my hands on it. My mother said that the book changed me. It was true.

The story was an autobiographical account. When Yu-pao was nine years old he wanted to go to school but he couldn't. His parents were peasants and deeply in debt. They depended on Yu-pao's labour. The family farmed on rented land and was barely surviving. Every morning while cutting grass and picking up firewood Yu-pao watched his neighbouring friends go to school. He was filled with envy. Sometimes he would sneak into the local temple where the class took place, peek into the window and listen to the class hours on end on his tiptoes. When the class was over he would practise writing using a twig to write in the dirt. One day the class was taking a field trip up to a hill. Yu-pao took his sheep and followed the class at a distance. During a break, the teacher, Master Zhao, gave the children a spelling quiz. No student was able to come up with a correct answer. Yu-pao, forgetting where he was and who he was, yelled out the right answer. Master Zhao was surprised. He called Yu-pao over and began to talk with him.

That night Master Zhao visited Yu-pao's parents and convinced them of the importance of education. When he promised to wave the tuition, the parents gave permission for their son to go to school. There was a paragraph which described the moment Yu-pao learned the news:

> That morning Yu-pao didn't have much spirit while working in the fields and he didn't collect much firewood either. He was depressed. When he got home, he unloaded the hay and firewood and sat down on the door-sill to take his breath. His sister, Yu-rong, saw him and ran out of the house. She shouted happily, "Yu-pao, you are going to school tomorrow!" Startled, Yu-pao said, "You must be kidding!" "Why should I? Go and ask Dad yourself!" Throwing aside his sickle and rope, Yu-pao got up and ran into the house. His mother was putting dinner on the bed—the bed at meal time was used as a table. Yu-pao hopped on the

table and pulled his mother's blouse, "Mom, please tell me Yu-rong is lying! Am I really going to school?" The bowl of porridge almost spilled over her hands. Mother said, smiling, "Look at you, do you have a manner of a good student?" "You all are kidding me!" "Nobody is kidding you. Come, Yu-pao, eat." Still Yu-pao couldn't believe his luck. He crowded over to his sick father, who was lying against the wall. "Dad, is it true?" "Yes, tomorrow, your mother will walk you to the school. Don't you misbehave. You hear me?"

After the meal, Yu-pao again didn't feel real about the news. He took Yu-rong aside and insisted on her reporting the details. He wanted to know how Master Zhao's visit went and how the parents were finally convinced. That afternoon Yu-pao went out and continued collecting firewood. He hummed songs, chased dogs into the fields and hens up to the roofs. He didn't stop until he collected bundles of firewood that would last for weeks and he collected a dozen bird-eggs while he climbed the trees …

Yu-pao's dream of going to school didn't last. Master Zhao was ordered by the town boss, a predator of Yu-pao's family debts, to remove

Yu-pao. I remember breaking down each time I read the departing scene. By the end, Master Zhao told Yu-pao never to give up studying and Yu-pao took the advice to heart—he became a well-known author after the Liberation.

I Want to Go to School had such an impact on me that I realized how privileged I was to be going to school, although I had trouble. My classmates laughed at me for I couldn't afford fine clothes. I wore clothes with melted sleeves and missing buttons and shoes with holes in the soles. Nevertheless, I reminded myself every day that I was going to school.

Jim Moore

The Salt Ecstasies—James White

James White died in 1981. His last book, *The Salt Ecstasies*, was published a year later by Graywolf Press. I knew Jim just well enough to take his work for granted, the way we sometimes do with friends. I knew he was a good poet, of course, but I didn't realize just how good until I reread *The Salt Ecstasies* after a reference to his work by Mark Doty, who said how crucial Jim's poetry had been to him at a time when there was very little poetry being published in America about being gay.

It's true that when Jim was finally able to write—and publish—poems about being gay, an intensity and urgency entered his work, both in terms of craft and subject matter, which had not been there before. But to say Jim's poems are about being gay is like saying Cavafy's poems are about being gay. True enough, but that's only the beginning of the discussion. Like Cavafy before him, Jim's poems are about everything that matters when we finally get down to business around forty or fifty: loneliness and longing; memory as a tug of war between regret and forgiveness; a newly treasured sense of dailiness; and acceptance. (Jim called this kind of acceptance "submission" in his brilliant series of poems, "Poems of Submission.")

In Jim's case, getting down to business included one more thing: the fact that he knew he was dying. Surely that awareness also was a factor in the urgency of the poems. But what could possibly account for their calm? When combined with the urgency, this calm allows the poems to enter a new landscape where devotion feels as natural as breathing. Here is a poem that emerges from that urgency, one written by a man who knew he was dying, who lived alone and with very little money in a modest apartment in an ugly and unforgiving city:

DYING OUT

I love the cambric night snowing down First Avenue
and the heaven of being near things I know,
my apartment, the old rugs and chair, the moons
of my nails above which I write.

And the snow in distant woods where animals
give silently all
and everything into dying—their fossils in spring,
the jonquil and pure bone.

I'm no more alone than usual
with this perfect history of snowing
so quietly without people.
I've left so many this year
who've felt too comfortable with my old design.
Because I want another life rinsed new in middle age,
the way a hard sickness changes a person.
The way snow changes the billboards
by my drugstore to read VANQUISH PAIN and
RELIEF FROM THE ORDINARY.

I don't want forgiveness from people,
only to be seen from another way,
like the back of a sculpture,
perhaps the nape of a neck or an open helpless palm,
some familiar form viewed from another direction.

Jim was every bit as neurotic and fearful as the rest of us. But in his poems there was a transformation which perhaps had to do with their music, his *submission* to it being so complete. He wrote a free verse of such easy mastery, with such clear and merciful rhythms, that I have to believe that when this music entered his poems, Jim followed its lead devotedly, a devotion which is at the heart of what makes *The Salt Ecstasies* a consoling book as much as a harrowing one.

How astonishing, one feels after reading *The Salt Ecstasies*, to be able to live in a world where a man can be dying in circumstances that provide very little shelter, and still write the twenty-two poems that make up this book, poems as much about America as about Jim, about the late twentieth century as the unknown mysteries we ascribe to words like "infinity" and "eternity," words that stand in for that feeling which arrives inside us sometimes when the boundaries inscribed by time give way completely.

The Salt Ecstasies is a slim book, twenty-two poems in all, and most of them quite short. There is no fluff here. This quality in itself (a quality enhanced by the editing some of Jim's friends helped with after his death) separates Jim's book from many others written during the last twenty years which are three times its length without a third of the passion. Despite its rigorous and unsentimental desperation, the book's assuredness of craft and vision is so complete it leaves only exultation in its wake.

Erin Mouré

The Fishes—Url Lanham

It was a book called *The Fishes.*

I think the author was "Url Lanham." A discursive book, with fuzzy black and white pictures, for children around thirteen or fourteen years old, about the history of fishes. I was in my twenties when I found it, in a bookstore on West Broadway in Vancouver, in a bin in front of the store, only one copy, either remaindered or damaged, I think. I thought that children at about fourteen, in the throes of puberty, should know about the history of fishes. It seemed directly to have to do with puberty. The only quote I still have from it is in a poem in *Search Procedures* called "The Life of St. Teresa." The quote: "Even if we could have been on the scene when the fishes developed lungs, we could scarcely have predicted the ultimate significance of the invention." I must still have had the book when I wrote the poem, but it's lost now. I lost it in 1995 when I lost a lot of things. Why fishes? I guess because of being asthmatic, I've often thought of the lungs as not very useful an invention. Only later I understood why lungs are so problematic: if you could spread them all out flat, they'd have more surface than the skin. But why get into that. I can still remember the book's pale green cover. I miss it. No one I knew was ever interested in reading it, or even listening to me talk about it, and I've been talking about it for twenty years now. I wonder where it got to. It was pretty scuffy. "The ancient and heavy fishes." All I know is that when you come home on a hot day and fill the kitchen sink with cold water and bury your head in it, the only noise you can still hear is what comes from inside; you know you're an organism then. And when you straighten back up to breathe, the water runs off your face in sheets of cold and streams right down your arms.

Susan Musgrave

The Name and Nature of Poetry—A. E. Housman

I FOUND JOHN COULTER in the Shannon airport, in the west of Ireland, May 1979. He lugged an antique typewriter plastered with CNR stickers, and I offered to carry it for him. We sat together on a plane to Toronto; he was 89, he said, and going home to settle down in Canada.

In the years before his death, at the age of 96, I visited him whenever I was in Toronto, at the apartment he rented on Avenue Road. John, a playwright, known on both sides of the Atlantic, had known the days, as they say in Ireland, and also the writers. He pronounced Yeats to rhyme with "beets," and told me James Joyce had stolen his walking stick, which was now on display in a Dublin museum. He intended to get it back. On one visit, after he had read some of my poetry, John loaned me a fragile little book called *The Name and Nature of Poetry* by A. E. Housman. This essay, which I have quoted from over the years—in my own essays and book reviews—captured the essence of what I had always understood about poetry, but had never been able to articulate.

Poetry is not the thing said, but a way of saying it, Housman wrote. "Even when poetry has a meaning, as it usually has, it may be inadvisable to draw it out."

"I hear you write poetry. Modern poetry. *That's* annoying," an elderly aunt (twice removed) shrieked at me when we were introduced. Housman's essay provided me with the perfect retort, one I've used often when confronted by an aggrieved family member or stranger claiming not to *understand* my poetry. First of all I quote Coleridge (as quoted by Housman) who said poetry gives the most pleasure when only generally and not perfectly understood, that perfect understanding will sometimes almost extinguish pleasure.

If that doesn't satisfy, I try this:

> The majority of civilized mankind do not possess the organ by which poetry is perceived. Can you hear the shriek of a bat? Probably not; but do you think less of yourself on that account? Do you pretend to others, or even try to persuade yourself, that you can? Why be unwilling to

admit that perhaps you cannot perceive poetry? Is it an unbearable thing, crushing to self-conceit, to be in the majority?

Most people will be stuck for an answer.

But then there are the professional critics, the ones who get paid, who want to know what your poetry means to mean.

Meaning is of the intellect, Housman says; poetry is not. He feels poetry is more physical than intellectual—causes a shiver down the spine, or makes the whiskers on the chin stand up (he must have believed civilized women did not possess the organ by which poetry is perceived, either). The best poetry, I think it can be agreed upon, horripilates.

Why can mere words have the physical effect of pathos? "I can only say because they are poetry, and find their way to something in man which is obscure and latent, something older than the present organization of his nature," Housman says.

I made a few notes in my journal (looking over them now, I see the ink has begun to fade), then returned the book to John, who said, "I should leave this to you." And in an unexpected way, of course, he did.

Michael Ondaatje

Bringing Tony Home—Tissa Abeysekara

When I first read *Bringing Tony Home* three years ago, it felt as if I had come across a book from my childhood, one I already knew well. It was of course my childhood I had come across, found evoked—with that strange, exaggerated sense of description ("as the woman disappeared inside the house I noticed she was frighteningly thin and flat like a steamroller had gone over her"), and enlarged sense of things, such as a too-heavy jug one was supposed to carry a great distance. The book had the delicious sad sense of being a solitary in the world, with a thousand intricacies between you and your closest neighbour or relative.

Bringing Tony Home was written in 1996 and is not a "lost classic," but I had the sense of having found one. Something about the way it was written, was slipped by accident into my hands, something about its quick disappearance and, in fact, its non-appearance in the West, made it one.

Title page of the paperback edition, 1998

"In the last years of the forties, when I had still not reached ten years of age, my family became desperately poor."

So begins *Bringing Tony Home.*

The author, Tissa Abeysekara, is a contemporary Sri Lankan filmmaker who in mid-life wrote this first novella or memoir about a disappearing moment from his childhood. It is a book written by someone roughly my age, about a mutual era of childhood. I had, till reading it, never found a book with such a physical echo of my life in Sri Lanka. Usually, I transpose the location and setting in any novel about childhood that I read so I can fit the events into a familiar place. For instance, as a boy in Sri Lanka I knew only one house with a staircase and so for many years whenever anyone in a novel climbed or descended the stairs, whether a Karamazov or the Count of Monte Cristo, they did so in my Aunt Nedra's house.

So Tissa Abeysekara's slim novel about a childhood loss took me right to the place of my youth. Not just to Sri Lanka, not just to Colombo, but specifically to the High Level Road in Boralesgamuwa. And there, in a place I knew and could recognize—and could slip into without translation—I was introduced to the people in his boyhood story, coloured and altered by the forty years of the author's adult life.

It is a simple story about a family that has to move because of a change in fortune and in doing so, it becomes necessary to leave behind the family dog. The boy, a week later, returns on his own to the village to look for "Tony," and because of the narrator's smallness, and because of the "largeness" of the world around him, the journey he makes is mythic. "The glass smelled vaguely of sardine and the water tasted like when it is taken from a galvanized bucket, but I drank it all in one breath and returned the glass to the woman with both hands...." I feel that already I am simplifying a privately heard tale. It is a book I wish to share only by passing it over to a reader. Funny and tender. Dangerous. Unfair. And of course it is one of the saddest stories.

What is wonderful is the way Tissa Abeysekara can make a whole era hang on a single strand of memory:

Each year during the April season a giant wheel would be constructed in Depanama and it would be there till after Wesak; this year they were constructing it on the little hill overlooking the Pannipitiya Railway Station where, once upon a time there was a tennis court, and every Saturday Father would come in the evening to play tennis with Messrs. Arthur Kotelawala, Bulner, Subasingha, and the Station Master, Mr. Samarasinha, and I would sit perched on the embankment by the cactus bushes with Guneris the servant boy and watch the trains come and go in the station below, and during the Sri Pada season which was from early January to late May, the trains were full of pilgrims and white cloth fluttered like bird feathers from the windows, sheaths of areacanut pods bristled, voices chanted and along with it the iron wheels of the train braked, clanged and screeched all blending together in perfect harmony and held together by the sad melancholy whistle of the train as it left the station and behind was the sound of the tennis ball hitting the racquet the ground or the net in a soft but clear and varying rhythm …

Then one by one they stopped playing; Mr. Subasingha disappeared because—I heard my mother and father whispering to each other—his wife had run away with a Tamil gentleman who was the Apothecary at

> the local government dispensary; Mr. Kotelawala had a stroke and was ordered complete rest; the Station Master, Mr. Samarasinha started drinking during the day also and was too drunk by evening to play tennis, and old Mr. Bulner simply stopped playing. We moved from the big house to the small one at Depanama and Father had no time to play for he left early in the morning on a bicycle and would return late at night even on Saturdays, and sometimes he would be gone for days. And the tennis court was abandoned and weeds grew all over it and the iron roller that used to level the court was dragged by some village boys to the top of the little hill and rolled down where it ended in a ditch and lay there like a broken animal.

The portrait of the world is farcical and formal in the way the author insists on giving us a torrent of details and names and everyone's official role, for children know and remember the labels on adults: the Apothecary, the Station Master. Because it is these details of society in his memory, blending together in perfect harmony, that once held his childhood society together. But the habits of parents, the memories of public fights, disappear and are discovered to be mutable—so it is a book not just of a child dealing with the loss of one dear dog but of everything, the whole world that surrounds his life.

Accordingly, the descriptions are detailed and frantic, an aria of lists that tries to hold the past together—in the way that the adult filmmaker in a subliminal sub-plot continues to make films, now in this region. "Forty-five years later I killed myself trying to capture something of this atmosphere in the opening scene of Pitagamkarayo, and the paddy field on which the final sequence was staged was the very same paddy field."

The tragedy within the book is not the loss of the animal *per se*, but the boy's awareness that he must in the end leave it. He is being forced to turn into an adult, which is the deeper sadness in this story. On a second reading we realize the boy in the story is looking back, so that contemporary opinions and events also flood in within this "slight" story, told in double time with young and with adult eyes:

> By eleven o'clock I had finished my assignments: rations from the coop store—the smelly yellowy big grained milchard; six chundus of it at two per coupon, sugar; brown sticky and smelling faintly like stale bees' honey: three pounds of it, Dhal: the variety referred to as "Mysoor

parippu," fine-grained and pink and mistakenly believed to be coming from Mysore in India and boycotted under the orders of the JVP when the Indian Peace Keeping Force was alleged to be raping girls in Jaffna in the late eighties until someone enlightened us that the dhal had nothing to do with India and was really "Masoor Dhal" which came from Turkey …

We hold onto favourite books for reasons that are not universal. Each word and sentence in this one carried me into arms I'd been in before. No other book brings me as close to my lost self.

It is a lost classic for me, too, because of the book's quick fate. Published in Sri Lanka by a small press it has so far not been published anywhere else. It was a story written far from the publishing centres of the West and there it remains, still lost to the rest of the world.

(Sri Lanka, 1988. ISBN 955-96434-0-1. Rupees 200)

CARYL PHILLIPS

Put Money in Thy Purse—Micheal Mac Liammoir

FOR OVER A YEAR, between January 1949 and March 1950, the Irish actor and director, Micheal Mac Liammoir worked with Orson Welles, having been cast by Welles to play Iago to Welles's Othello. *Put Money in Thy Purse* (a quote from *Othello*) is a brilliant account (in the form of a dairy) of the difficulties of making the film. By the end of the book one is left in no doubt as to why the studio system ultimately failed this maverick, Orson Welles. In fact, one is left wondering how Welles ever got his madcap career off the ground in the first place.

The tale begins with Orson Welles sending a telegram to an ailing Mac Liammoir, demanding that he immediately leave his sickbed in Dublin and fly to Paris for a screen test. Welles is sure that a mere sighting of "Orson Welles" will undoubtedly cure the Irish actor of his various ailments. Mac Liammoir remains unconvinced. Although some fifteen years have passed since the two last met in New York City, Mac Liammoir clearly has some inkling of the chaos to which he might be exposing his life. He and his partner, Hilton Edwards, the director of the Gate Theatre in Dublin, enjoy a well-ordered domestic and professional life that is centred around the Irish theatre. However, curiosity eventually gets the better of Mac Liammoir and, having convinced himself that he will be finished with *Othello* by the summer and thus able to return to the theatre, he answers the maestro's call.

During the course of a week of "testing" in Paris, Mac Liammoir learns that there has already been some filming with another actor playing the part of Iago. In fact, filming has been going on for quite some time, the interruptions occurring only when the money ran out. A confused Mac Liammoir returns to Dublin, and silence. "No word from Orson, and wonder if my film career at an end. Cannot make up mind if joy or sorrow would ensue if it were." Welles eventually rescues Mac Liammoir from this state of ambiguity and summons him back to Paris and then to Rome, where he subjects the poor Irishman to a month of chaotic "rehearsals." Mac Liammoir has difficulty fathoming just what is going on, for disaffected actors are constantly being replaced by a director who, somewhat disconcertedly, keeps disappearing. It becomes clear to Mac Liammoir that

Welles has assembled the cast and crew of an international production without having secured proper financial backing, and without having even the most rudimentary sense of schedule. In short, Welles is simply making it all up as he goes along.

Having endured a week of frustrated isolation in Rome, word eventually reaches Mac Liammoir that Welles is now in London, and that he'll soon be flying to Morocco to make an entirely different film. Mac Liammoir is offered the choice of waiting for Welles in Rome or in Paris, of going back to Dublin, or flying to the Moroccan desert to join him. An exasperated Mac Liammoir flies back to Dublin, but six weeks later finds himself on a plane bound for Casablanca and more "rehearsals." Once there he learns that Welles has now abandoned plans to shoot *Othello* in Rome and Paris, and that once Welles is finished with his current project they will apparently be making *Othello* in Mogador, a small town on the west coast of Morocco that contains no hotel. Welles's personal assistant informs an astonished Mac Liammoir that, "Orson will probably take a villa where you will all be one happy family." Having only just arrived in Morocco, Mac Liammoir is then instructed to return to Paris and "wait there."

Filming eventually begins in Morocco. As fate would have it, the very first scene that Welles shoots with Mac Liammoir is illustrative of the chaos that has dogged the whole production. Unsurprisingly, none of the costumes have arrived in Morocco from Rome. The scene that Welles wishes to shoot is one in which an attempt is made on Cassio's life by his friend Roderigo, who is subsequently murdered by Iago. The scene traditionally takes place in the street, but after a sleepless night "the winged gorilla" (as Mac Liammoir now calls him) decides to film the murder in a steam bath, with the participants stripped and draped in towels. This "inspired" decision not only solves the costume problem, it suggests an intimacy between the characters which makes the treachery all the more disturbing. Welles's technique often calls for similarly bold improvisation, but not always with the same degree of success. For instance, his decision to shoot, and then dispense with, two different actresses in the role of Desdemona, before shooting with yet a third actress, inevitably creates much frustration among both cast and crew.

During the course of filming there continue to be a startling number of unscheduled "breaks" in order that the director might fly off in search of more money. At such moments, the crew and cast, at enormous expense, are abandoned in various locations, often for weeks on end, idling, reading,

Orson Welles (right) as Othello

sightseeing, sniping at each other, and wondering about the many contractual obligations that they are now jeopardizing. But somehow, through sheer force of personality, Welles manages to hold the ship steady. Over a year after receiving the original telegram, Welles turns to the author and says, "Mr. Mac Liammoir, I am happy to tell you you are now an out-of-work actor. You have finished Iago." One can almost feel Micheal Mac Liammoir's huge sigh of relief rise up from the pages of his book.

Put Money in Thy Purse reminds the reader that there was a time when cinema was an art form in which the director was the supreme artist, and the actors—however famous—were merely strolling players. Throughout the length of this book there is barely a mention of agents, managers, publicists, lawyers or accountants. Welles not only manages to convince his "team" of the supreme importance of this production of

Othello, he even has them planning future productions, including a world tour of various theatrical classics, and a film of *Julius Caesar*. For all his eloquently expressed ambivalence about the current project, even Mac Liammoir spends a couple of days of yet another unplanned "break" cutting the text of *The Importance of Being Earnest* in the hope that the play might be included in the world tour of theatrical classics.

Orson Welles—actor, director, producer—a man of immense charisma and supreme stubbornness, illuminates the book. But ultimately, *Put Money in Thy Purse* is Micheal Mac Liammoir's book and, through the eyes of this civilized and intelligent actor, we are able to see how an artist learns to trust that which he does not always understand, how he grows to tolerate that which he initially disliked, and how he comes to recognize strength of character where he first espied only weakness and folly.

Micheal Mac Liammoir (left) as Iago

And what of the final film? Well, although Micheal Mac Liammoir's text ends with his own "wrap," and quite some time before the shoot was over, we now have the evidence of the complete and edited film to set beside the book. As it turns out, Orson Welles's *Othello* is one of the truly great transpositions of Shakespeare to film. It is full of shadowy suggestion, unusual camera angles, big close-ups, and dazzling montage; it is Shakespeare as *film noir*. Welles knew what he was doing—artistically, that is. But then again, so did Mac Liammoir; his outstanding performance is a key part of this remarkable film. He chose to rise from his sickbed and answer the call of Orson Welles; but luckily for us, he chose also to write about the improbable, and often hilarious, obstacles that daily confronted this troupe of believers as they made their masterpiece under the guidance of "the winged gorilla."

Cassandra Pybus

The Dead Seagull—George Barker

I WAS BLOWN AWAY when I first read *By Grand Central Station I Sat Down and Wept* back in 1967. I had just turned twenty and saw myself as a martyr to passion like Elizabeth Smart, "shot with wounds which have eyes that see a world all sorrows mortally pierced with the seeds of love." Her vision of tormented love spoke directly to me. Of George Barker, the poet she had read and then obsessively tracked down and seduced, I knew nothing. Browsing the bargain pile in a cut-price bookshop one day I caught a glimpse of his name on the cover of a slim paperback. Furtively flipping the pages I was astounded to read that Barker was describing the exact same passionate travail as Smart. But with such loathing, such untrammelled vitriol. It made my cheeks burn with rage. Nevertheless I bought *The Dead Seagull* for next to nothing, which was just as well since I have never heard another thing about this book.

Smart first published *By Grand Central Station I Sat Down and Wept* in 1945 and Barker *The Dead Seagull* in 1950. In the mid-sixties they were re-published within a year of each other. Since then Smart's book has stayed in print and become iconic for several generations of susceptible young women, while Barker's seems to have disappeared without trace.

Barker and Smart did read from their books together at a writers' conference in Glasgow in 1980, half a lifetime after the passionate folly that engendered the books (and their four children). I am pleased not to have been there to see it, since these two extraordinary prose poems do not belong to the world where rash mortals grow old and find themselves performing curious rituals for a voyeuristic public.

Well yes, their story can easily read as banal: a marriage destroyed by a passionate compulsive affair; a woman so obsessed by desire for one man that she become shameless and ruthless, though ultimately martyred to her passion; a man unable to choose between saintly wife and wanton lover, who is destroyed by lust. In the hands of Smart and Barker the tawdry tale undergoes poetic transmutation into grand myth: "Jupiter has been with Leda and now nothing can avert the Trojan Wars" we read in *By Grand Central Station I Sat Down and Wept*. In *The Dead Seagull* the self-lacerating narrator recognises the object of his desire as "pig-woman,

Circe" from whom he cannot break free, and his passion "a field of wild oats that would one day spring up fully armed and destroy me."

The writing in both pieces is compelling: visceral and poetic at the same time; a precise and condensed rendering of emotions as raw as an open wound. Each has been dubbed a masterpiece of poetic prose. Yet what makes these two small volumes remarkable, for me at least, is not the astonishing poetics or the pagan eroticism, but the relentless solipsism. In each book nothing exists but the tortured self: "Everything begins, as its ends, with the egoistic heart," Barker writes.

No wonder they so little understood each other.

Here is the possible reason why one survives in triumph while the other is lost. Elizabeth Smart's readers, I suspect, are like me at twenty: ready to be swept up in her vision of a transcendent passion which obliterates the obligations of conventional morality. On the other hand they are likely to be repulsed by the Janus face Barker presents. His narrative is shot through with disgust: at himself for his lust and at Smart for her greedy, amoral, animal passion, "tearing my life to rags."

The central image of the book belongs to a dead gull Barker finds on the beach, the perfect metaphor for his virtuous and betrayed wife. Placing his hand upon the bird's breast—symbol of his wife's broken heart—he spits out a curse: "Gull the bitch." He means them both: the suffering wife and the rapacious mistress between whom he shuttles back and forth in a rage of indecisive self-disgust. What he really longs for is to be free of his need for women. He dreams of becoming hermaphrodite.

I was both compelled and repulsed when I first read this. How could Elizabeth Smart have got him so wrong?

Yet it is all there in *By Grand Central Station I Sat Down and Wept* where Smart describes her lover as "the hermaphrodite with a golden indeterminate face." And she hears him plainly enough shout his fear and disgust from the tangled sheets of their adulterous bed: "You're a cunt. Nothing but a cunt." But through the prism of her overweening solipsism Smart sees only what she wants. Just as Barker sees only what he fears.

The Dead Seagull was written while Barker and Smart were still harnessed together in their tortuous sexual bargain. The narrator claims to be writing in 1945 and addresses himself to his son, called Sebastian, the name of the second child Smart had by Barker, born in 1945, the very same year she published *By Grand Central Station I Sat Down and Wept*. Smart was to have two more of Barker's children in the next two years. "Every time I sneeze, a child is conceived," his narrator ruefully confesses. It was a kind of curse he believed.

By Grand Central Station I Sat Down and Wept is undoubtedly a classic and *The Dead Seagull* is its lost half. One is incomplete without the other. Strange no one has thought to put them together in one volume, though god knows who would have the stamina for such an overload of reckless self-obsession.

Andrew Pyper

The Good Soldier—Ford Madox Ford

What makes a "great novel"? Iris Murdoch has taken as good a stab as anyone at naming the criteria by demanding it be a story that provides "something for everyone." By this Murdoch didn't mean pandering to satisfy a broad audience, but the synthesizing of every rhetorical tool available to the writer to create a new and particular world that somehow also gives us a sense of the universal. By this definition, *The Good Soldier* is a great novel. It is also a piece of art that brilliantly hides as much as it reveals.

Thankfully, *The Good Soldier* is a classic that is not entirely lost. But it is under-read and egregiously under-taught, principally, I suspect, on account of its greatest asset: its elusiveness. Interpreting *The Good Soldier* is such a rewardingly tricky business because it is ultimately "about" its refusal to present directly to the reader what novels, up until that early point of the twentieth century, had been obliged to hand over: the true motives, emotions and verifiable actions of its characters. Instead, we get only the unreliable point of view of the novel's narrator, the impotent (in every sense) John Dowell, whose buried hatreds and comic layers of denial threaten to reveal themselves as the story progresses.

And what is the story? On its surface, *The Good Soldier* tells the tale of two marriages, of Dowell to Florence (who "represented a real human being with a heart, with feelings, with sympathies, and with emotions only as a bank note represents a certain quantity of gold"), and of Leonora to Captain Edward Ashburnham ("You would have said he was just exactly the sort of chap that you could have trusted your wife with. And I trusted mine—and it was madness.") Marriage, however, stands here as an institution of intimacy and trust that just as often demonstrates the opposite of those qualities. Yet the point of Ford's critique is not to show up the rottenness of these particularly spoiled couples, nor to prove the bitter impossibility of love. That would be far too neat and final. What the author uses his four deceivers to show more than anything is the deceptive nature of the human heart, which has a way of betraying its owners as much as the hearts of others. The end of Captain Ashburnham may well be, as Ford subtitled his novel, "The Saddest Story Ever Told," precisely because the tragedy is of such a pitiably small scale (two pampered couples keeping secrets at a German spa), yet no less affecting for such downsizing. The incomplete communications, every unheard whisper and interruption, all anticipate the fractured condition of human discourse we would later qualify as the postmodern. As a work of political criticism, it is one of the most powerful fictional illustrations of the disappearance of honour among the elite classes who, heading into the First World War, hadn't a clue as to how much their sense of order and propriety was about to be unhinged. And the writing itself is at every instant absolutely what it must be: strategic, inventive when the moment demands it, wholly assured in its voice, and funny in the saddest possible way.

The Good Soldier is a book of lies—adultery being the least of them—that in turn makes us uncertain of our own groomed and polite surfaces. I feel *bad* every time I read it, as though I have participated in its web of fakery and loathing myself. But it is precisely this self-critical effect that drew me to Ford in the first place, the way he flies below the radar in order to knock out the reader's usual defences of distance and superiority. The good soldier of the novel is good, if we judge only by first appearances ("So well set up, with such honest blue eyes ..."). Yet he is something far less than that if we care to look more closely ("I had forgotten about the eyes ... When you looked at them carefully you saw that they were perfectly honest, perfectly straightforward, perfectly, perfectly stupid. But the brick pink of his complexion, running perfectly level to the brick pink of his inner eyelids, gave them a curious, sinister expression ..."). The same eyes—the same character—at once sinister and good.

But I take Ford's unstable "good" to be applicable not just to Edward Ashburnham but to us all, to some uncomfortable measure or another. Doesn't every one of us sometimes say exactly the opposite to what we really mean? Don't we sometimes know this, and say it anyway? This punishing irony is most effectively delivered by *The Good Soldier*'s Dowell, whose final exclamation of love for his "good" friend Ashburnham—like our own society's self-congratulatory claims of sharing, caring and community—may as well be a hiss of barely concealed contempt.

MICHAEL REDHILL

Lependu—Don McKay

THERE WAS A TIME in my life when I knew almost nothing about the writers of my own time or place. I was introduced to poetry in grade school and high school in the way most Canadians of my vintage were: when it came time to wade through the poetry "module," a large survey of antique writers were rapidly explicated by teachers who had no particular love of the writers or the poems. And, at the end, there was a test to see if you could break one of Shakespeare's sonnets into feet and draw in the rests and stresses.

Although by this point it was widely believed in my high school that people had stopped writing poetry after about 1950, I was lucky enough to have a teacher who smuggled in Ginsberg, Olsen, Creeley, Atwood and nichol. We were shocked that it was entirely possible that there were poets living in our own city. After this class, and starting in university, I began to rifle the poetry shelves in used bookstores. One of my happiest discoveries was a thin collection of poems called *Lependu* by Don McKay.

I don't remember exactly where I turned this book up, but I do know the copy I own is the only copy I've ever seen. These are the first lines:

> When Lependu loves you
> he's the shadow they discover on your lung
> that whets each breath.

I can't explain why these lines hit me like sock in the gut, but they did and they still do. Like McKay's later work, *Lependu* is a wild roil of lyricism and goofball comedy; wordplay and unkempt syntax that hits the reader like jazz on the ear; and there's a deep, abiding sense of history and nature too, as in all his work. (*Lependu* is about, among other things, London, Ontario, and McKay even draws us a historical plaque on page six, which he says is "stuck like a thought balloon in the city's comic strip.")

McKay mixes straight prose with poetry (slipping from one form to another like a man busting into drunken song), and the sacred with the profane. *Lependu*—the title means "the hanged" and refers to Cornelius Burleigh, the first man ever hanged in London—reset my poetic North.

McKay just lets it fly in these pages, it's mayhem. You come across murderers, dainty ladies, Tom Thomson, phrenology, the London Life Insurance Company, and the trickster Lependu him- (or rather it-) self, who swims and swans through it all, the devil taking the fiddle. The sheer gusting power of the language knocks you back, as McKay filters an awe-some range of impulse and energy through the poems:

Back and forth salaam salaam the sprinklers
graze and pray on plush
carpets of grass, beer becomes sweat, the heavy
air surrounds, mothers us to immobility, the mind
melts, the elements
slump, four fat uncles in their lawn chairs, while the flesh
well the flesh just ambles into town to get drunk with the ball players.

I just can't believe that McKay wasn't shouting whoa! whoa! as he wrote this, at least I hope he was. Look at that "salaam salaam" there in the first line. Onomatopoeia meets sight gag. I see those sprinklers bowing low in wet obeisance with their greetings of peace in the midst of such heat, not to mention the four elements transubstantiated into "four fat uncles" … man, it makes me want to cry.

Lependu was published in 1978 by Nairn Publishing of Coldstream, Ontario. It's never been reprinted. *Lependu* made me want something for myself as a writer, the first book to do that for me. The fact that it's so hard to find, and therefore not enough read, is sad considering that McKay is still very much alive, and it would be wonderful if more people could tell him what a great book it is. (Although the chance to appreciate McKay is regularly presented: his most recent book, *Another Gravity*, builds on the promise of *Lependu*. Where else but in McKay's work do "…Chestnut-backed Chickadees kibitz and flit…"?) Anyone who is lucky enough to come upon this lost classic of Canadian poetry will identify with Christopher Columbus (a *Lependu* cameo) who "walking through his newfoundforests/ whispers *mama mia* to himself."

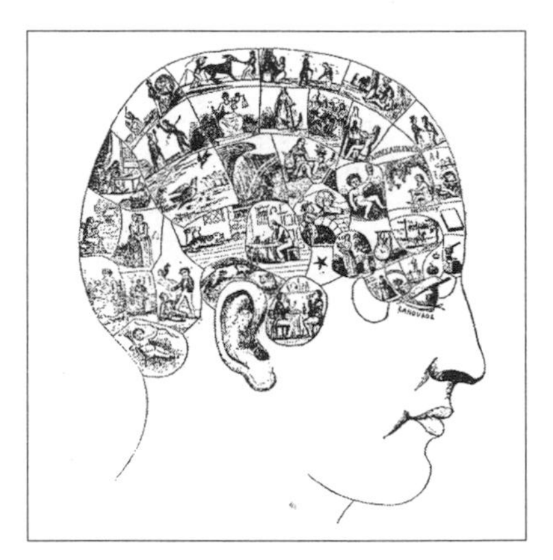

Frontispiece illustration from the Nairn Publishing House edition, 1978

Bill Richardson

The Mouse and His Child—Russell Hoban

While Christmas shopping, I went to a store that sells cute robotic animals. The activated beasts—rabbits, cows, sheep—were contained in a small corral. They all marched in the same direction. When the leaders of the pack met the fence, it stopped them in their tracks. The animals behind butted up against them. Bottlenecked, the only motion they could achieve was an up and down kind of humping. An obscene daisy chain. A sexualized version of a peaceable kingdom. The lions didn't just lie down with the lambs. They knew them, carnally.

These were the waning days of 1999. This rubbing together of plush loins seemed a symbol for the awful gang-bang of a dying century. Mass production and mindlessness. Circuitry and carnality. Could it be that their dangerous governance accounts for the flirtatious relationship *The Mouse and His Child* has had with Books in Print? At the core of Russell Hoban's novel are precepts antithetical to those that have reigned over us.

It is about individuality and independence of mind. It is about proper clockwork and what it can do.

Hoban, among whose books are *Riddley Walker* and *Turtle Diary* and *Pilgermann*, is one of a handful of writers who publishes widely for both children and the withered. His first books, illustrated by his then-wife Lillian, were for very young readers. Perhaps the best known are the little stories about a badger named Frances. By the time *The Mouse and His Child* came along, in 1967, Hoban's books for little folk numbered fifteen. The novel, his first, tells the tale of a clockwork mouse and his son. They are on a quest to find both a family and the secret of becoming self-winding. Of course, *The Mouse and His Child* was caught up in the slipstream of Hoban's reputation and published and promoted as a children's book. Which in some ways it is. But which in most ways, strictly speaking, it ain't.

Here's how it starts. There's this clockwork toy, the eponymous (eponymouse?) mouse and his child. Father and son are joined at the hands. When wound, they dance in a circle. The big mouse lifts the little mouse up and down. It's Christmas time. They are among the wares on offer in a toy shop. They share shelf space with a lavish doll's house and a seal who balances a ball. Presiding over the whole is a hoity-toity society dame of an elephant. The toys inhabit a universe regulated by the immutable Laws of Clockwork. It is Paradise, ripe for losing.

The mouse and his child are sold. Years go by. The son never forgets the doll's house. He never forgets the seal, whom he thinks of as his sister, or the elephant, whom he regards as his mother. One day, disaster strikes. The mouse and his child get wrecked. They are discarded. Homeless and alone, it looks like things can't get worse. But they can, and they will, as they make their long and dangerous journey back to Paradise.

En route, they encounter Manny Rat, a malevolent force who salvages wrecked wind-ups and uses them as slave labour. While fleeing that nemesis, the mouse and his child variously fall in with a frog-cum-seer; a traveling theatre company, The Caws of Art, run by a couple of crows; with a philosopher and playwright named C. Serptina, who is also a snapping turtle. They endure trial by fire, by water. They become hardened and wary. They become warriors. But they never lose heart, never lose sight of goodness. In the end, the Paradise to which they stake their claim is leagues removed from the one they lost, but sweeter for being the one they made.

If, in spite of enthusiastic reviews and an animated film adaptation,

The Mouse and His Child has been more often out of print than in, it is surely because it defies classification. It is no more for children than is Hans Christian Andersen. It is no more for adults than is *The Odyssey*. It is a book that is right for whoever is ready to read it. Intricate, funny, violent and allusive, it is a witty amalgam of Homer, Grimm, Wittgenstein and Beckett. Hoban has said in interviews that he didn't have children first and foremost in mind during the writing, and the young readers who will relish its complexities will be as scarce as those adults who find satisfaction in reading books written—or at least marketed—for children.

The miracle, I suppose, is that it was published in the first place. Mind, that was more than thirty years ago when publishers resonated to a different aesthetic and a different kind of economy. With its cranky resistance to category, and its hard edges, it would astonish me if anyone would take a chance on *The Mouse and His Child* today. Happily, it is already there, and the other miracle is that, one way or another, in print or out, it will continue to find its way into the hands of readers of whatever age who for whatever reason want or need it. For it is a moveable monument. For it will always travel. For by now, it is self-winding.

Eden Robinson

The Twilight of Briareus—Richard Cowper

When I was in grade nine, some well-meaning souls decided to try out an experimental English class. In an attempt to nurture creativity I suppose, we were allowed to read anything we wanted for class, as long as we kept lists of what we'd read. The first week, I tore through eight books. The second week, ten. The third week, I dropped to four—it was the J.R.R. Tolkien's *The Hobbit* and *The Lord of the Rings* series. I'd gobbled down the trilogy in one weekend, reading straight from Friday night to Sunday evening, bursting into tears when I finished because it was over and I was back to boring old Kitamaat Village where it rained three hundred days out of the year and most conversations started out with a discussion of how good or bad the fishing season was going.

My English teacher—a harried man with piercing black eyes and thirty students who used his class as an excuse to goof off—called me to his desk. "Look," he said. "This list is supposed to be books you've read, not books you want to read."

I felt my shoulders collapsing. "But I did read them."

"Can you describe any?"

I didn't know where to start. He pointed to a book on the list and asked what it was about. I mumbled something about the plot, the characters. He pointed to another book. And another. And another. I started to expand, describing my favourite parts, passages that blew my mind, the way I wished the books had ended. He waved me back to my seat.

After that day, I couldn't help myself. The second the roll call was over, I'd run to his desk, clutching my latest find, describing page by page what I'd read. I'd follow him around the class, babbling, while he tried to talk to the other students.

I'd gone through almost the entire science fiction and fantasy section of the library when I found Richard Cowper's novel, *The Twilight of Briareus*. Radiation from a nearby supernova renders most of mankind sterile and causes global climate changes. Aliens riding the supernova shockwave help repopulate the earth, but their solution destroys the qualities that make people human. The breadth of Cowper's imagination, the delicacy of his characterizations, the unpredictability of his plot—I couldn't verbalize these then. I thought it was the coolest book I'd ever read, and since then, I haven't read many science fiction novels that equal the originality of *Twilight*'s dark vision.

In class, I didn't even wait for roll call. I pulled a chair up to my teacher's desk. He leaned one arm on his chair, put his hand over his mouth and watched me with his eyebrows raised high as I told him about *Twilight*. When I finished, he said I didn't need to give him reports any more. He'd believe anything I put on my list. I waited for him to say something else, and when he didn't I slunk back to my desk, disappointed—now I'd have no one to talk to about books.

Twilight's out of print, but I saw it in a used bookstore once. The joy of finding it was tempered by the memory of that moment in class when I discovered that not everyone shared my enthusiasm for science fiction.

LEON ROOKE

Geraldine Bradshaw—Calder Willingham
The Tenants of Moonbloom—Edward Lewis Wallant

THERE ARE TWO BOOKS I've been carrying around for the last forty years. Both are by novelists once celebrated, now mostly forgotten.

Born in 1921 to the Georgia Willinghams (the Willinghams are an old and prominent Southern US family), Calder Willingham published his first novel, *End As a Man*, in 1947. The novel—uneven, occasionally brilliant, frequently powerful—grew out of a year the author spent as a cadet at the Citadel in Charleston, South Carolina, before transferring to the University of Virginia. The book was well-received, though not by the Citadel or Calder's family. The school brought suit against the publisher and a much-publicized trial was held. Later on, Calder adapted the book to the stage; three film versions are said to exist, *The Strange One* being the best known.

In 1950 Vanguard published Willingham's second novel, *Geraldine*

Bradshaw. The next year *Reach to the Stars* and *The Gates of Hell* (stories) appeared, and the year after that, *Natural Child*. Through the next three decades other well-travelled Willingham novels surfaced: *To Eat a Peach, Eternal Fire, Providence Island, Rambling Rose* and *The Big Nickel*.

The Willinghams had long since given up on the prolific author. A Tennessee cousin who carries the same name tells me that the family, likely traumatized by the controversy surrounding *End As a Man*, distanced themselves from the writer, viewing his work as pornographic.

Their attitude is all the more amazing when one considers Calder's extensive movie work, not the least of which was his screenplay collaboration with Buck Henry on the benchmark film *The Graduate*, for which the two received an Oscar nomination. Other movie credits include *Paths of Glory, One-Eyed Jacks, Little Big Man*, an uncredited collaboration on David Lean's *The Bridge Over the River Kwai*, and the screenplay of his own novel *Rambling Rose*.

Willingham has said he regarded his fiction as his "real" work. Hollywood work was done to support his wife and six children (he married twice). Sadly, these days film is the sole medium that preserves his writing. The novels have been long out of print.

My favourite among the books is the funny/sad, powerfully invigorating, language-flying, roller-coaster *Geraldine Bradshaw*. Willingham was always good with women characters, and Geraldine is a mercurial creation of the first order. The trouble with Geraldine is that she is forbidden by the gods to tell the truth. The truth she must not tell is to the party lusting after her through 415 pages, one Dick Davenport, a bellhop at the Manchester Hotel, Chicago, 1943. The lie she must tell has all, or mostly, to do with her virginity, or lack thereof. The lie is life, we might be saying, and if it is not life, then it is certainly story. Few can invent, out of one mouth, so many stories so convincingly, so startlingly, so beautifully, as Willingham can. Part of the wizardry for the reader of this novel is figuring out with Dick what Geraldine's true story is—and knowing in the meantime that loving her is good for the son-of-a-gun Dick's own meandering—lying—character.

Note: Calder's father was a hotel manager in Atlanta. Two of Calder's novels and several stories have hotel bellboys as their heroes. You'd think his father would have appreciated that.

Calder, sad to say, died in 1995.

Edward Lewis Wallant was born in New Haven in October 1926, was dead in December 1962. Cerebral aneurysm, coma. Age, thirty-six.

After his day job, he worked nights in a rented room, in four years producing four novels, minor-to-major classics, two of them published posthumously.

With his first two, *The Human Season* and *The Pawnbroker*, critics, with good reason, were already speaking of him in the same amazement with which they beheld Malamud, Mailer, Bellow, Salinger, Roth.

Nowadays he is all but forgotten, his books out of print (though Syracuse University Press's Library of Modern Jewish Literature may bring some of them back).

In the last year of his life, Wallant completed *The Tenants of Moonbloom*. It was his final book, although in publishing sequence it appeared to be his third. Both it and *The Children At the Gate* were published posthumously.

If we regard the sixties in the American states as a period burdened with disillusionment while simultaneously being jacked-up by hope, we may say *The Tenants of Moonbloom* perfectly captures both.

At the beginning of the novel, Norman Moonbloom, still a virgin at 33, the perpetual student (accounting, art, literature, dentistry, the rabbinate, podiatry), is a year into his first job. He is a rental agent for his brother Irwin's four crumbling Manhattan properties. In these properties reside a diverse citizenry to which Wallant will soon allow full voice: Jewish, Black, Chinese, Italian, other. Moonbloom arrives each week to accept his tenants' money and record their displeasures: toilets backed up, leaky roofing, wiring "so bad the inspector wouldn't take a bribe," unsafe elevators, black halls, rotting railings, holes in the floors, rats, cockroaches. In old Basellecci's apartment the wall by the toilet defiantly bulges, a "swelling tumour." Brother Irwin fears a tax hike; he wants no repairs beyond the minimum.

Tenants see Moonbloom as humourless, passionless, a man underwater, faceless, a man asleep. Moonbloom sees himself the same way. "He walked through the evening streets to the subway at Fourteenth Street. The sky arched into superfluous immensities of distance; for Norman, the distance between him and the nearest passer-by was infinite."

But hold on. Gradually, Moonbloom makes entry into these people's lives, and they into his. The world rearranges itself. Thus we enter the last astounding forty pages. Moonbloom personally restoring the properties. Any sentimentality here? Not a whit. These final pages—at the very end Moonbloom tackles the tumorous wall—must be considered as among the most joyfully uplifting, the most ennobling, of any penned by a serious talent.

Like Calder Willingham, Wallant is a master in rendering the human voice. Too bad Calder is no longer among us. He could turn Wallant's classic into a great movie.

JANE RULE

The Peterkin Papers—Lucretia P. Hale

THE PETERKIN PAPERS WAS FIRST published in 1886. My own copy, snagged from my parents' library when they were divesting themselves of family detritus, is a third edition, published in 1928. It was for my brother and me one of those books which were always there, not for reading but for being read to, even long after we needed aid, simply for the pleasure of our mother's voice. Even now, sixty years later as I skim its pages, I hear my mother's voice, expressive, amused, anticipating the familiar and satisfying conclusion of each chapter.

The Peterkins are a family made up of an enterprising father, over anxious mother, one daughter, Elizabeth Eliza, and a variety of sons, including "the little boys in their India rubber boots" always rushing off to help solve a family problem. The problems are simple: Mother has put salt instead of sugar in her coffee; Elizabeth Eliza's new piano is delivered and placed with its back facing out into the living room; the horse refuses to move. But the solutions are as complicated as all the suggestions anyone in the family can offer. For the coffee, first the chemist is sought. When he fails, the herb lady is called in. When she fails, the little boys set out once again to what is always the family's choice of last resort, the Lady from Philadelphia, a frequent visitor to the town, who offers the solution, "Make another cup of coffee." Elizabeth Eliza spends the summer playing her piano by sitting on the porch and reaching the key board through the window, but as winter comes on, she and the family are getting colder and colder. Consulted, the Lady from Philadelphia suggests turning the piano around. With her opera glasses from her own window, the Lady from Philadelphia can see that the much cajoled and abused horse needs to be untied from the hitching post.

The Peterkins seemed to me not so much feckless as amateur, adults and children alike, as attractive in their eager resourcefulness as they were silly. Though it was easy to feel superior to them, it was reassuring to know that other families made mistakes, got into trouble, and finally solved their problems with a little kindly help. It was the Lady from Philadelphia, however, who was the book's main attraction. Unlike our own grand-parental advisors, who gave orders rather than offering advice, who never waited to be asked, the Lady from Philadelphia was a patient oracle who only responded to requests and never mocked or scolded, simply solved the problem. Though I couldn't have put it into words at the time, she was also American without title, without magical powers or the immortal weight of myth. She was my first role model. Though I've said for years we only need bad ones to teach us what not to be when we grow up (scolding, criticizing, interfering grandparents), I know as I sit in my chair reading or at my desk writing, I have half an ear cocked for the sound of India rubber boots on the path, the knock at the door, and I hope that my advice is as simple, useful, and kindly as the advice of the Lady from Philadelphia.

JOANNA SCOTT

Genoa—Paul Metcalf

FROM *THE NEW YORK TIMES*, Late Edition, Sunday, January 31, 1999: "'Like a medieval chronicler with the eye of a poet and the heart of a tale-teller, he fits together radiant fragments into a wholly new kind of construct,' the author Guy Davenport once wrote of Mr. Metcalf ..."

... who, among other things, was the son of Eleanor Thomas Metcalf and the great grandson of Herman Melville as well as a descendant of Roger Williams, the founder of Rhode Island, and who as a child in a distinguished New England family was educated at private schools and then, predictably, attended Harvard, but he disliked it there so much that he left after just three months. He married Nancy Harmon Blackford of Charleston, South Carolina in 1942, lived in the South for twenty years, and in the early sixties returned with his family to the Berkshires, where he wrote (compiled? arranged? orchestrated?) *Genoa*, one of his best-known works yet on the endangered list of cultural memory—

—a book I found in a used bookstore in Rochester, New York. I bought *Genoa* because it was signed by the author and I bought a worn paperback edition of *The Egoist* because I'd recently come out of a conversation feeling ashamed that I hadn't read anything by George Meredith. A decade has passed since then and I still haven't gotten around to *The Egoist*, but I started *Genoa* that night and read with growing astonishment.

There are no recalls, no flashing images, no digging in and rooting of the body—rather, the beginning of a journey such as I have never before taken.

During the ice age, Metcalf informs us, the ice covering much of North America was sometimes two thousand feet thick. A waning moon is good for shingling, because it pulls the shingles flat. And a girl should never marry until she can pick clothes out of boiling water with her fingers.

Did you know that pasted to the inside of Melville's desk and discovered after his death was this slogan: "Keep true to the dreams of thy youth"? Or that, in Paul Metcalf's estimation, the "forward progress of the human spermatozoon is at the rate of about 1.5 millimetres a minute which, in relation to their respective lengths, compares well with average swimming ability for man"?

Or that Melville once wrote about Hawthorne, "Still there is something lacking—a good deal lacking—to the plump sphericity of the man"?

There are few fictions that make information so startling, so pleasurable. *Genoa* is a collage, or a symphony, "with the sources like old diaries and botanical descriptions as the different instruments" (his daughter Adrienne's words). Metcalf bombards us with facts, dazzles us with quotations and mimicry, weaves together bits and pieces of a fictional narrative about two brothers—Michael Mills, the club-footed guide of the book, and his doomed, dangerous brother Carl. *Genoa* takes as its subject the greedy process of inventive thought. To make something new we must accumulate information and consider, if not fully comprehend, the possibilities of association between unrelated subjects, such as:

1) An early edition of Melville's *Mardi*

2) Gray's *Anatomy*

3) *The Hoosier Schoolmaster* by Edward Eggleston

4) *Cosmology* by H. Bondi

5) *The Search For Atlantis* by Edwin Bjorkman

6) The March 1952 issue of *Natural History*

7) Textbook of Embryology

8) *Journal of Morphology*

These are the books Michael Mills keeps on his desk. He spends his time considering these books. He thinks about his brother's crimes. He thinks about Columbus—

"There was the man from Genoa, who went to sea at fourteen and ..."

He quotes Melville: "I have a sort of sea-feeling, here in the country, now that the ground is covered with snow."

Christopher Columbus. Herman Melville. Paul Metcalf in *Genoa*: "... there is this about Columbus and Melville: both were blunt men, setting the written word on the page and letting it stand, not going back to correct their errors, not caring to be neat."

The mind groping. Hah! Oh! Yes, yes. What? The unbelievable stuff of this world. Columbus and Melville. The ice age. The forward motion of spermatozoon. Hawthorne. Ahab. Billy Budd. A club-footed narrator and his degenerate brother. Indianapolis and St. Louis. The web of fiction and fact. Emerging from Genoa for the first time, I felt perplexed by the minutiae in the room—everything deserving observation and contemplation, everything potentially revealing but in bulk overwhelmingly puzzling. And then the interruption of time. This to do, and that, and …

… *The New York Times*, Late Edition, Sunday, January 31, 1999: "Paul Metcalf, who made his mark as an experimental writer of prose, poetry, and plays, died on January 21 near Pittsfield, Mass. He was 81 and lived in Chester, Mass. His wife, Nancy, said Mr. Metcalf had a heart attack after buying apples at a farmers market not far from Arrowhead, the Berkshire home of Herman Melville, his great-grandfather."

Paul Metcalf on *Genoa*: "I have written a wicked book, etc., etc."

Sarah Sheard

Down and Out in the Woods: An Airman's Guide to Survival in the Bush

I'M WINGING IT ON the subtitle, unverifiable until spring, when my parent's cottage reopens. The one battered and rain-fluffed copy I know of is archived there. Haven't come across another yet. This manual of food, shelter and first aid was the companion text of my childhood summers, inspiration for countless scavenger hunts, bandaging orgies, and the rape of birches for lean-to thatch.

Fresh cattail roots can be roasted and eaten, the book informed. Their taste is mild and sweet, not unlike potatoes or chestnuts. They can also be ground into flour for pancakes. Mosquitoes (a nutty taste) will, if consumed in sufficient quantity, maintain a man due to their high fat content, unlike most other insects, save grubs—which can be found by aping Mister Bear and clawing open rotten logs. To yield a nourishing meal quickly, whole patches of grassland can be set alight and combed through afterwards for roasted insects and vermin. A meter-square patch can yield as much as a cupful of edible insect protein. Potable water can be collected by filtering urine through a pant leg, tied off and filled with sand. Spruce needle tea wards off scurvy and makes a refreshing drink, year-round. A stretcher can be created using two stout branches and a buttoned-up pair of shirts; a dislocated shoulder set using a forked stick and a leather belt. Makeshift armour against biting insects can be fashioned from birch bark and shoved down socks. Fresh river mud dabbed elsewhere does a good job. And so on.

Some of the book's first aid tips have since been debunked. Snake bite, I understand, is no longer treated by razoring through the punctures and sucking out the venom, which induces worse trauma and risk of infection than lying very still until help (or death) comes. Tourniquets in the hands of amateurs are now contraindicated, risking greater morbidity of flesh than the haemorrhage they're designed to staunch.

Moss, Nature's compass, grows on the north sides of trees (although moss around my family's cottage grew on every which side, disoriented from years of proximity to Sheard psyches.) Harvesting a cattail root was tricky. My brother and I paddled upstream, leaned over our canoe's gunwale and tugged. Nothing budged. Furthermore, I was afraid to step into marsh water for leeches, edible though they were. With great effort, we uprooted a handful with our paddles but they were scarcely bigger than a finger and remained persistently tough and parsnippy even after hours of patient roasting (cheating with foil) in the oven. Grinding them into a powder between two stones yielded a smear of shreddy pulp and stone grit. No potato. No flour.

Down, but not yet out, Sis and I carved a shallow fire trench around a patch of spindly grass growing between the driveway ruts. We set it alight and thumbed through the scorched earth for bug bodies. We came up with a thimbleful of sooty black pips that may have been grass seeds or ants, and an earthworm, spiralled and hard as a bedspring. The birch-bark shin-guards proved effective but they tickled and worked loose. Needle tea was a bitter turpentine.

To rally the troops, my father laid his long arm across the picnic table at twilight, a human filling station for mosquitoes. My siblings and I watched with horrified admiration as he tongued up the first blood-bloated customer with much smacking of lips and eye-rollings of relish. He must have downed ten or twelve of them before my mother intervened. My father complained of feeling fullish, due to the fat content, no doubt. I wondered about malaria.

Down and Out extolled the virtues of self-sufficiency and transcendence over squeamishness, transforming any natural landscape into a smorgasbord of edible *Where's Waldo*. Romanticism was the condiment that added savour to these otherwise unpalatable wisdoms. In adolescence, alongside these rustless treasures in my mind, I feverishly laid up survivalist tips to other activities, like dating and sex: Girls, carry a little mad money in the finger of your glove and: always keep one foot on the floor. The tips accumulate still on money, career and the heart.

The downed airman within me walks through the shadows of the valley of life armed with delusions every bit as precious as those from its pages claiming that cattail roots taste like potatoes and a trouser leg of sand can change urine into wine.

Eleni Sikelianos

The Granite Pail—Lorine Niedecker

The poet Anselm Hollo gave me two of the most important gifts I have ever received. One was a folded photocopy of Alice Notley's "Homer's Art"; the other, for my twenty-fifth birthday, Lorine Niedecker's *The Granite Pail.*

> Remember my little granite pail?
> The handle of it was blue.
> Think what's gotten away in my life—
> Was enough to carry me thru.

The next morning, I took *The Granite Pail* into the backyard—an abandoned orchard still full of plums and apricots, and pears and apples, each in their proper season. It was late spring, and rocket flower bloomed up around my knees as I sat in the grass and opened the book.

Something in the water

like a flower

will devour

water

flower

The day was warm and blue, planes buzzed overhead, and soon every detail of the morning converged down into the book as the poems rose—really rose—off the page. This was a voice that knew people—that was warm. Over the years, Niedecker's work became a guide for me. From her, I learned to throw *things* to the flood (a great antidote in these times), to pay close attention to all parts of the poem—sound and thought, layout and image—and to jettison the unnecessary parts into the waters.

Today, I have dragged my computer out of the dark back room and onto the kitchen table and am looking out into a bright, chilled fall day in Manhattan. There are no orchards for miles around, though there are morning glories on the fire escape, which have gone brown and bedraggled. In the next room, amidst other books of poems, is my copy of *The Granite Pail*, ticketed with red flags (each with its own timeline and geology) to mark the pages I love.

> 'a laborinth of pleasure'
> this world of the Lake

The book went out of print long ago and Niedecker's work is still hard to find, though there are other collections available now. But, for me, nothing will compare to this edition, which has taken me through years of reading and, most recently, to the shores of Lake Superior, where I saw Niedecker's locks and white castleworks, and where the gulls did indeed play "both sides" of the water.

Sam Solecki

On Being Blue—William Gass

ONE OF THE LAST books G. Wilson Knight published was called *Neglected Powers*. I've always liked the title, even wished that I had come up with it. Thirty years after reading the book, I no longer remember, with the possible exception of T. F. Powys, the powers that Knight considered neglected, but I suspect that the book nudged me into keeping my own casual list of undervalued or nearly forgotten books and authors. Over the years, some that were once on the list have gained the readership they deserve; Bulgakov's *The Master and Margharita* (1966–67) is one. Others like Cunninghame Graham's *Mogreb el-Acksa* (1898), which inspired Shaw's *Captain Brassbound's Conversion* and was praised by Conrad, and Ramon Guthrie's collection of poems, *Maximum Security Ward* (1970) have sunk even further into oblivion. Still others like Arthur Koestler's autobiography or Zbigniew Herbert's first collection of essays (*Barbarian in the Garden*) await a wider audience.

The presence of William H. Gass's *On Being Blue* on this list seems to confirm that the various books have only one thing in common: me. Gass's book is about blue with roughly with the same inflections as Stevens's *The Man with the Blue Guitar*. With the exception of a section discussing various philosophical theories of perception, the book is a beautifully written, loosely organized meditation on the word's various meanings and uses.

> Blue pencils, blue noses, blue movies, laws, blue legs and stockings, the language of birds, bees and flowers as sung by longshoremen, that lead-like look the skin has when affected by cold, contusion, sickness, fear; the rotten rum or gin they call blue ruin and the blue devils of its delirium; Russian cats and oysters, a withheld or imprisoned breath, the blue they say that diamonds have, deep holes in the ocean and the blazers which English athletes earn that Gentlemen may wear; afflictions of the spirit—dumps, mopes, Mondays—all that's dismal—lowdown gloomy music, Nova Scotians, dyanosis, hair rinse, bluing, bleach; the rare blue dahlia like that blue moon shrewd things happen only once in, … the shaded slopes of clouds and mountains, and so the constantly increasing absentness of Heaven

(*ins Blaue hinein* Germans say), and consequently the color of everything that's empty.

Casual, playful, witty, and serendipitous, Gass lingers several times over "blue words" and our failure, in life and literature, to find a language supple and expressive enough for sexuality. He is a stand-up comedian when explaining why we resort to "Go fuck a duck!" but avoid "Go fuck a fox!" "Go fuck a trucker!" His list of invented insults includes "May your cock continue life as a Canadian." He becomes Rodney Dangerfield when he lists coinages of his own that have not passed into daily use: grampalingus, meatus foetus, mulogney, squeer, crott, kotswinkling, and papdapper. Shaking his head in disbelief, he reminds us that "We have a name for the Second Coming but none for a second coming. In fact our entire vocabulary for states of consciousness is critically impoverished." The fascination with the word and the inability to stop worrying it gradually reveals itself as the sign of Gass's love of language and his desire to approach life by way of what James calls "the country of the blue," that is, the imagination. For Gass, we fail in sex and in life when we fail to be attentive to, even to love language which, in a manner of speaking, is the imagination incarnate, the Word become the word. Or, in Gass's post-Christian view, the words on the page are the only Word we have to describe caressingly what the aptly named Wordsworth calls "the very world, which is the world/ Of all of us, the place where in the end/ We find our happiness, or not at all!" And his style is itself an act of imaginative attention.

> If any of us were as well taken care of as the sentences of Henry James, we'd never long for another, never wander away: where else would we receive such constant attention, our thought anticipated, our feelings understood? Who else would robe us so richly, take us to the best places, or guard our virtue as his own and defend our character in every situation? If we were his sentences, we'd sing ourselves though we were dying ... it's not the word made flesh we want in writing ... but the flesh made word.

The sixteen thoughts that Gass says he has "on being blue" are stretched across an axis at one end of which blue is the colour of our despair, while at the other it is the colour of the imagination and of what-ever redemption may still be available to us.

… the use of language like a lover … not the language of love but the love of language, not matter, but meaning, not what the tongue touches, but what it forms, not lips and nipples, but nouns and verbs.

Esta Spalding

Lost Horizon—James Hilton

SALINGER'S *FRANNY AND ZOOEY* opens with Franny leaving her boyfriend, Lane, waiting at their restaurant table, contemplating his second martini, while she goes into the bathroom, pulls a pea-green clothbound book from her coat pocket, and moves her lips, reciting the lines. The book is *The Way of a Pilgrim*, and the lines she recites she hopes will enter her heart so that her body—her very heartbeat—will become a prayer.

At fifteen, when I first read Salinger, I saw myself in Franny. Her questions were my questions, her fears, my fear. But the book I chose to carry was a different pilgrim's way. For me the book was James Hilton's *Lost Horizon*, a thin, paperback volume given to me by my mother. She had seen the movie, she said, when she was my age, and it had changed her life. I took this to heart, discovering in *Lost Horizon* certain secrets that I can no longer remember. I know those secrets echoed the very ones discovered by Conway, the book's hero, during his brief sojourn in

Shangri-La. While Conway is there he is able to explain to his fellow travellers the mysteries revealed to him by the high Lama:

> He narrated rapidly and easily, and in doing so came again under the spell of that strange, timeless world; its beauty overwhelmed him as he spoke of it, and more than once he felt himself reading from a page of memory, so clearly had ideas and phrases impressed themselves.

Once Conway leaves, he cannot find the words, the way back to that place. This loss is one part of Shangri-La's mystery. The other part—as Conway and his companion, Lo-Tsen, discover when they attempt to leave—is immortality. While in Shangri-La, Lo-Tsen is as young as she was the day she arrived fifty years before, but reaching the summit of the last peak on her way out of the valley, Lo-Tsen suddenly grows old: her spine withers, her skin wrinkles. Outside of Shangri-La, time returns, and Lo-Tsen's body betrays her.

During the months of that difficult fifteenth year I carried *Lost Horizon* with me on my daily journeys, and from time to time would pull it from my backpack (growing up in the tropics, I did not wear a coat) and open the familiar pages to lines that were heavy with meanings capable of answering questions, fighting fear.

Another fifteen years have passed. I keep a copy of *Franny and Zooey* at hand and read it every couple of years. Because I have read it so frequently—in different bedrooms, under various light—the book does not seem to have changed. Or we have changed together. As for *Lost Horizon*, until last year, I had not read it in all that time, but I had moved it with me from city to city, apartment to apartment. The old paperback had even survived a basement flood that left its spine swollen, its pages yellow and wrinkled. When I opened the book, a few months ago, it was with trepidation but the certainty that it was time. I began to remember the joy I'd felt

The Pocket Books edition, 53rd printing, 1963

in its simple and clear lines, its assured and wise narrator. I felt again the chilly thrill upon the first sighting of Shangri-La, and the further thrill of the lama's revelations. In this reading, I appreciated the beauty of Hilton's craft, but I could not remember why, at one time in my life, those words had seemed necessary as breath. That place was lost to me. I had grown older, after all.

Linda Spalding

The Ten Thousand Things—Maria Dermout

I FOUND IT IN A remainder bin and chose it for its cover, which looked tropical and haunted. The places I have loved in books are inevitably smoky, sea-gripped, time-laden. Musk and damp pervade. People are controlled by fate. So it was that opening this accidentally discovered book, I came upon a spice garden in the Mollucas and was transported.

It is the story of a "small woman" in a batik sarong and white cotton jacket living her life in a water-lapped garden inhabited by the living and the dead. I read it years before I made my own trip to the Indonesian archipelago, but I had lived a long time in Hawaii and was nostalgic for my garden there and for the two children I had tended in its shade, now almost grown. "It seemed as if the garden took the two children away and hid them: in all the water, the cistern, the rivers, the shallow inner bay; in all the green, the trees, the wood, the rosebushes on the hills and the forests behind the hills at the foot of the mountains—once they lost their

way there and were found in the dead of night only, by a torchlight party."

The dead inhabit this story, although people—several generations overlapping—are less conspicuous than vegetation and less important than sea and sky. There is an earthquake during which part of the house collapses on a mother and child. There are murders: three young sisters, all poisoned on the same day, who still come to the garden to play and leave little piles of shells on the sound. There is the historical Rumphius,

Three editions. Facing page: Simon & Schuster, 1958 (left), University of Massachusetts Press, 1983. This page: Aventura, 1984

a botanist who lived on the island of Ambon in the seventeenth century. The small woman reads his books and keeps a cabinet of curiosities just as he did. In it are shells and potions. Its drawers hold time as well as precious things. Then there are visists from the *bibi* who brings things to trade including necklaces of tears, both from the earth and from the sea. She is ordered away when she drapes the small woman's child in the necklace of head-hunters from Ceram, announcing his tragic fate.

Maria Dermout was born on a sugar plantation in central Java in 1888 and wrote this first novel at the age of sixty-seven. Published in Holland in 1953 under the title *De Tienduizend Dingen*, it was translated into eleven languages … then disappeared. According to the dust jacket of the

American edition I now have, she had lived in "every town and wilderness of the islands of Java, Celebes and the Moluccas." Having moved to Holland after the war, and after losing her only son, she, too, was nostalgic.

Lately, there is something else. I never imagined travelling to Indonesia when I first read *The Ten Thousand Things*, but now familiarity thickens the plot. Ghosts and potions, head-hunters and wet forest. "Trees everywhere, even in the water; at the bay, beside the swamp covered with lilac water hyacinths, were rows of gleaming little nipa palms and somber mangrove trees on their tortured bare trunks. Sometimes there were sea snails on the branches, under convex white shells, like porcelain fruit." I have been led to blind Rumphius, too, and his book *The Ambonese Curiosity Cabinet*, where I read about snakestones, red crabs and the poison-wood trees that are exactly as Dermout describes them, as if she has given his botanical specimens their own stories. As if they are sentient.

In this short tale of a young woman who comes back to her grandmother's garden to raise a child and grow old, Dermout shapes both lament and celebration. There is such a stream of characters—planters, soldiers, princes and thieves. But each of them harbours the "hundred things" that are, in those islands, called up at the end of a life: events, objects, remembered words, beloved people and places, "your beautiful house, your china dishes hidden in the attic, the swift proa, your sharp knife, the little inlaid shield from long ago, the two silver rings on your right hand, on index finger and thumb, the tamed pidgeon; but also, hear how the wind blows!" A son murdered by the head-hunters of Ceram. Three ghost-sisters playing on an empty beach. The curiosity cabinet and its contents. As the story circles on itself, they number in the thousands, so that anything once loved is eternal, beautiful, unchanged.

Lawrence Sutin

A Fool's Life—Akutagawa Ryunosuke

At a library sale in the late 1970s, I found a copy—crudely stamped "Officially Withdrawn" and suffering from a tattered binding—of *A Fool's Life* by Akutagawa Ryunosuke. Less than a decade after this Grossman Publishers edition had first appeared—with stunningly fine tipped-in etchings by Tanaka Ryohei—it was being cast off on the grounds both of its physical condition and its lack of appeal to library patrons.

I was faintly familiar with Akutagawa as the author of the short story "Rashomon," upon which the famous film by Akira Kurosawa is based. I had read that story and found it rather contrived and constrained. But I took a chance on this copy of *A Fool's Life* as it was cheap and wounded and lovely.

I read it in a single sitting—no particular feat, as the memoir consists of fifty-one brief chapters, some as brief as three sentences. I was at the time eight years younger than was Akutagawa when in 1927, at age thirty-six, he took his own life through a Veronal overdose shortly after completing *A Fool's Life*, the manuscript of which lay alongside his deathbed. Attached thereto was a letter to his friend Kume Masao, to whom—as had Kafka, tacitly, to Max Brod—Akutagawa left the decision as to whether it should be published.

I mention these somewhat sensational details because I seek to draw readers to *A Fool's Life*. But the fact of Akutagawa's suicide was not what made his book, for me that evening, a kind of soul-quake from which I have never recovered. What overwhelmed me then and still does was that Akutagawa had conveyed the entirety of a deeply lived life in fewer words than I would ever have thought possible. Virtually each of the chapters is a masterstroke of concision and revelation. (The translator from Japanese to English, Will Petersen, must take a bow here as well.) What Akutagawa showed me that night was that language possessed a greater tensile strength, depth of resonance, and relation to truth than I had ever before managed to realize.

In chapter forty-nine, "Stuffed Swan," Akutagawa described the writing of the book—an artful *trompe l'oeil* retrospective upon a narrative that had yet, in fact, to end:

> Drawing what strength remained, he attempted an autobiography. It was harder than he had imagined. Self-importance and skepticism and calculation of advantages or disadvantages were all in him. He despised this self of his. At the same time he couldn't help thinking, "Remove a layer of skin and everybody is alike."

It was Baudelaire, a particular favourite of Akutagawa, who laid down the gauntlet for modern memoir with his journal entitled *My Heart Laid Bare*. To reveal the uttermost secrets of one's depths is the risk, the lure, the brazen come-on of memoir in these times. Akutagawa—uncomfortable with so-called "confessional" literature, then enjoying a sizable vogue in Japan—chose the task not of laying bare the heart but of removing, with his surgical style, the skin of social concealment (the uniquitous lies by which he and we live), thus revealing, more searingly than Baudelaire in his journal, the nakedness of the fool huddled within.

In his letter to Kume Masao, Akutagawa wrote: "In the manuscript, consciously at least, there is no attempt to justify myself." One can argue that any personal writing is inherently an act of definition and hence justification. But by the human standards with which we may judge even writers, I will grant Akutagawa his claim and my homage.

Sharon Thesen

By the Sound—Edward Dorn

Edward Dorn's novel, *By the Sound*, while not exactly lost, was out of print for a couple of decades. It was reprinted in 1991 by Black Sparrow Press, which had published it for the first time in 1971; and it is, I think, a classic of a certain genre of prose writing that grew out of the poetics of the Black Mountain school, which was itself based on, somewhat back of that, the prose style of people like Edward Dahlberg, one of Charles Olson's mentors. Fielding Dawson comes to mind as another practitioner of this local and particular down-to-earthness, with strange torques and interventions that betray the author as, if one can use a word like this any more, "essentially" a poet.

Ed Dorn grew up in less than adequate circumstances in Illinois in the 1930s and became the author of many books of poetry, most notably *Gunslinger*, and a few of prose, his other novel being *Some Business Recently Transacted in the White World*. He lived in Boulder, Colorado, and taught in the Creative Writing department at the University of Colorado. He died in December of 1999.

By the Sound is by no means a great novel, but I remember that when I first read it, twenty-five years ago, I had never read anything quite like it. The story takes place in the early '60s in the Skagit Valley on the Washington coast near Puget Sound (hence the title, which also plays on "by ear") in a locale and a climate seldom presented in fiction as a real and ordinary place (as opposed to a surreal and extraordinary one: think *Twin Peaks*). The characters in Dorn's novel, two itinerant families, the Wymans and the McCartys, are forever on the verge of being down and out. Seasonal employment, like picking peas and beans for local farmers at harvest time and intermittent construction work, keeps them going. Between seasons they go to the "unemployment office" for pointless and humiliating interviews with bureaucrats:

> The interviewer ... put the lighter back in his pocket and blew the smoke out the side of his mouth and looked at the card again with his chin and his cigarette in the air. He went back to a bank of files. Mr. Hendersson and the little man stood and waited, watching. He returned with a sheet in his hand

saying, 'No, it's about the only thing here, but it's not the right kind of a job for this man, in the first place you have to have a car to get there, and besides that, it doesn't pay enough. This man has twelve kids.'

The Wymans and their friends the McCartys are constantly changing addresses, often the subject of charitable donations, and not completely reliable owing to poverty and a quite realistic absence of ambition. Ramona, one of the two main female characters, is an Eskimo who has lived in Seattle; Mary, her counterpart, is bookish and thoughtful. Digging clams at the beach and drinking at the While Away tavern are major pastimes. The men hunt deer in the fall, at night, for food; and the Mr. Hendersson mentioned above is eventually killed in an accident while working in a tunnel on a hydroelectric dam project.

Hardly a barrel of sparkling laughs—yet the novel does have a wry and knowing wit, and Dorn has a gentle touch. In a preface written for the 1991 edition, Dorn writes, "*By the Sound*, masquerading as a 'novel,' is simply a sociological study of the basement stratum of its time: the never-ending story of hunger and pressing circumstance in a land of excess." It's a quiet piece of writing, as quiet and unpretentious as its characters; and skimming it again the other day, so many years after I first had read it and enjoyed it mostly because it was a "poet's novel" of the time, though without much beauty, if any, maybe because of that lack of beauty, it now seems flat and a bit boring—Carver without the dynamics—but still, somehow, rather marvellous and necessary. And Dorn's preface to the 1991 edition is alone worth the price of the book: a wildly sardonic, apropos little essay on economics and culture.

Colm Toibin

❦

Forbidden Territory—Juan Goytisolo

I CANNOT FIND THE BOOK and the two or three people to whom I might have lent it have no memory of it, have never heard of it. But I have a clear memory of a Saturday in the summer of 1990, during a year when I tried to live one month in Dublin followed by one month in Barcelona and managed not to live much at all, but spent my time oddly disentangled, disengaged, suspended. And the book hit me hard. I remember late on a Saturday night, in a tiny room in a flat near Santa Maria del Mar realising that if I did not put this book down I would finish it that night, and when I woke in the morning I would not have it.

I put it aside and slept and then woke with the absolute and uncomplicated pleasure you normally get from finding a delightful and half-forgotten bloke in bed beside you. I started reading again and I am still recovering, in certain ways, from what I learned.

The book is Juan Goytisolo's memoir *Forbidden Territory*, which was published in hardback by Quartet in England. I don't know if it ever made it to a paperback. Goytisolo was brought up in bourgeois Barcelona, where the upper middle classes have remained undisturbed for a hundred and fifty years. Neither world war, nor the Spanish Civil War have had much impact on them, except to make them conservative in ways that are almost exquisite. As a child, Goytisolo was sexually interfered with by his grandfather, and as an adult, he is determined that the sort of sexual repression which led to this will not govern his life, but rather become the source of his liberation. His mother Julia Gay was killed by a bomb during the Civil War when he was a small boy (he was born in 1931) and that sorrow and a strange guilt, as anyone who has lost a parent in childhood will know, follow him everywhere.

He goes, as all good Catalans go, to Paris and there he meets Jean Genet who asks him straight out if he is a homosexual. Goytisolo is a provincial; his editor Monique Lange, who will be his lover for many years, is also in the room. He cannot answer; he hesitates. Maybe he is a homosexual. And later he tells us that at the time of writing the book he spends half the year with a working-class Moroccan man. It is complicated, so he cannot answer straight, but he feels shame about this, and Genet has no more time for fear and shame and prevarication.

I love the dark truths which Goytisolo is prepared to explore in the book. He is the boy who suffers alienation from family and Catalan society, who suddenly realises that, elsewhere, alienation—it is Paris in the 1950s—has become the new enlightenment. But this is not a cure, merely an explanation and, at times, a comfort. The damaged self is alone in this book; the aim of the journey is to know and explore the damage because it cannot be repaired. Things must be faced, and this is something I wish I could come to terms with.

Goytisolo realised that the enemy lingers in the language itself, and that language remains, no matter who else has used it, a soft wax when you are alone in a room with it. His novels are a great roar against the Spanish tradition since 1492, against grammar and syntax, as much as inherited boundaries and notions of culture and civilisation. The first volume of his memoirs set the context for this: he is uncompromising and honest not about the things which it is easy to be uncompromising and honest about—Franco's Spain, bourgeois life—but about the forbidden territory of the self, the things we wish to keep hidden.

Lola Lemire Tostevin

The Junior Classics: The Young Folks' Shelf of Books

My lost classic was a series of volumes actually called *The Junior Classics: The Young Folks' Shelf of Books*. Each volume contained classic stories retold to make them more accessible to a child. My mother bought them for me shortly after I was born and kept them at the back of the closet until she could read them to me or until I could read them myself. I loved them, each one a different colour—bright orange or red or purple—with gold-on-black lettering on the spine. A few had watermarks and mildew spots because a water pipe in the wall of the closet had broken and damaged the books before they were removed from their box. But it didn't matter. They were special. Unlike the few other books in our house—a French encyclopedia, a few dime novels, a couple of French and Latin missals—*The Junior Classics* had been written specifically for me. And they were in English. For some reason, I must have considered this an asset.

There were, I believe, ten volumes. In the one entitled "Stories That

Never Grow Old," I read abridged versions of Sir Walter Scott's novels and encountered, for the first time, conflicts between nations and cultures: Christians and Muslims in *The Talisman*; Saxons and Normans in Ivanhoe. Amidst vivid descriptions of magnificent flagged pavilions where tournaments and jousts were held for knights to show off their skills, and of galleries spread with Persian and Turkish carpets and tapestries for the ladies, cultural and historical wars never seemed that serious somehow. They were only the backdrops for the making of heroes.

The same qualities united all heroes in all volumes: to always speak the truth, to always keep a promise, to be constant in love, to be modest and gentle in heart, to help the weak and never take unfair advantage. These were the ideals of an age, and "chivalry" the word that expressed them. The first time I became aware of a connection between languages was in the volume, "Heroes and Heroines," in which I learned that the word "chivalry" came from the French "cheval," a horse.

Long after I had put these stories behind me, while visiting the Musée Rodin, in Paris, I found myself standing before an imposing and intense sculpture of six men, their faces rough-hewn, their hands and feet enormous, their bodies and stances powerful. They were simple, modest people, but Rodin's dramatic dimensions enhanced their power and their suffering. It asserted, like no other sculpture I'd ever seen, the dignity of the common man. The piece was called "The Burghers of Calais."

Suddenly it all came flooding back: a speech by a man called Jean de Vienne, the governor of a besieged town who, when called upon by the king of England to surrender unconditionally, replied something to the effect that the townspeople were ready to endure far more than any man had ever done before they would consent to harming even the smallest child. Six men had then come forward and offered their lives to spare the town. The story, "The Noble Burghers of Calais," was from one of the volumes of my *Junior Classics*, "Tales of Courage and Heroism."

The Bookshelf
for Boys and Girls

Prepared under the Supervision of
THE EDITORIAL BOARD
OF THE UNIVERSITY SOCIETY

VOLUME VI
Famous Stories and Verse

THE UNIVERSITY SOCIETY, INC.
Educational Publishers since 1897
NEW YORK

Title page from The Bookshelf for Boys and Girls, *Volume VI, published by The University Society, 1955*

I did enquire a few times if these volumes were still available but I never found any. Perhaps it's just as well. Rodin's sculpture summed up his transformation of the past into a monument that was contemporary and personal. I had read my simplified classics at an age when I was still moved by knights-to-be. Clothed in white, taking their oaths and being handed their spurs, their coats of mail, armlets, gaüntlets and swords.

In time, in spite of the volume "Stories That Never Grow Old," notions of heroism, courage and chivalry do change according to personal and contemporary perspectives. I doubt very much I would perceive the qualities that ran throughout these stories with the same innocence and unquestioned zeal.

Michael Turner

The Bells of Russia—Alexander Moskoyov

The name of the book is *The Bells of Russia*, and it was written (in English) by my babushka's second husband, an international lawyer named Alex Fishman, who self-published the book (in hardcover) under his Russian name, Alexander Moskoyov, just before he died, in Los Angeles, in 1967. I have never read the book—nor has anyone else in my family. According to my mother, the opening sentence is 576 words long.

I first came upon *The Bells of Russia* when I was seven. It was wedged between my mother's cytology textbook and my father's private school annual. I removed it from the shelf and took in its cover: a black-and-red drawing of a man in profile, probably my dad's age, on his knees praying. Around his neck, a manacle; around his wrists, chains. He was surrounded by fire. I showed the book to my mom and announced that I was going to start reading immediately, that I had no doubt it was a classic. She took the book from my hands, told me I was too young.

The next time I came upon *The Bells of Russia*, I was twelve. My babushka had just arrived from Los Angeles to look after us, while my parents, who clearly weren't getting along any more, left the country in an attempt to save their marriage. As a ploy to get our minds off my parents' troubles—I'm sure that was the reason—my babushka gave my sister and me a twenty dollar (US) bill and commissed us to write her a story. It could be about anything we wanted—as long as it was about Russia. Being a smart ass, I went looking for *The Bells of Russia*. The idea was to plagiarize something from the middle pages, that part of the book I was convinced most readers forgot.

After a couple of days of searching, I found it under a flat of plum preserves. I took the book upstairs to my room, flipped it open, and began my transcription. Suddenly, my mom walks in. Before I could say anything, she grabs the book from my desk and tells me, once again, that I'm too young. I told her I was five years older than the last time I was too young, and when was I ever gonna be old enough to read *The Bells of Russia*? That's when I heard about the opening sentence. It knocked the steam out of me.

When I was seventeen years old, my sister came home from school with a new boyfriend. His name was Hy, and he'd just arrived from Montreal. I was making something in the kitchen when Hy walked in, introduced himself. There was a strange, sonorous voice coming from the living room console. I knew it wasn't something from our collection. I asked Hy if it was his record, and he asked me if I liked it. I told him I did. Hy left the kitchen and came back with the sleeve: *The Songs of Leonard Cohen*. I looked at the picture of Cohen, then looked at Hy. Identical—same nose and hair. Then I flipped the record over and saw what looked to me like the cover of *The Bells of Russia*. Only this time it was a woman in flames, not a man. And she had chains around her wrists, too! The perfect couple, I thought. I spent the next hour rummaging through the house, looking for the book. When my mom came home from work I asked her where it was; where's *The Bells of Russia*? She told me my father took it with him when she kicked him out. Haven't seen it since.

Seán Virgo

The Amateur Poacher—Richard Jefferies

Richard Jefferies died young and bewildered in 1887, a failed novelist and half-baked philosopher. He wouldn't have chosen this book to be remembered by. But it is wonderful: as history, as social document, as a manual for poaching (fish, fowl and fur), as the creation of a world you can breathe and feel. And his style is his own.

It's partly the way he dispenses with bridges. "There are days in spring when the white clouds go swiftly past, with occasional breaks of bright sunshine lighting up a spot in the landscape. That is like the memory of one's youth. There is a long dull blank, and then a brilliant streak of recollection." His story moves without contrivance, from one sunlit spot to the next. Sometimes he switches focus completely in mid-paragraph, with no segue or apology. At twelve I found this natural and riveting. Today it seems masterful, co-opting the reader from the outset.

They burned the old gun that used to stand in the dark corner up in the garret, close to the stuffed fox that always grinned so fiercely. Perhaps the reason why he seemed in such a ghastly rage was that he did not come by his death fairly.

Rereading this today, I realize that that opening, which cast its spell when I was twelve years old, does not draw breath for another page and a half, and in that brief compass evokes a whole world—the values, lifestyle and economics of a doomed rural life, with the spectre, even, of emigration—though it seems just to follow a boy through the dusty treasures and terrors of an attic.

Interesting, the British books which start out under the rafters (think of George Macdonald's *Lilith*, with its mirror; Virginia Woolf's *Orlando*, with the dried Saracen's head). The attic of an old house is its memory, and Richard Jefferies had that attachment to place and history, and to the small wild creatures which the ancestors also knew, that is the saving grace of the Anglo Saxon psyche.

I was loaned *The Amateur Poacher* by my cousin Paul, a cool and glamorous boy, maybe six years my senior, who always had hares or rabbits or salmon to sell in the back lane. He slipped it to me one afternoon with a wink. It was my passport.

I was an alien in that scaled-down northern country, where a wooded coombe held the *mana* of a great forest, where two miles of peat bog seemed as vast as the High Veldt of my childhood, and where the whole land was cloaked, the dense air quickened, by—by what I could not tell. Now I made my way through that attic and down to the fields and "Everywhere under the flowers," I read, "are the dead."

Kids know how to filter the stuff they can't use out of adult books, but I read every word in that little blue book, several times over. I recognise those words today; I hear the cadences surface in my own work.

Thomas Hardy must have read the book when it was serialized in 1879 in *The Pall Mall Gazette*. The flatland village of Essant Hill, derived from "D'Essant-ville," with it's ancient church "whose space was reduced by the tombs of the Dessants," is surely the germ of Tess, and the same sense of history brooding over progress pervades the Wessex novels. Hardy's human range, with its conscious irony, was far beyond Jefferies', but he never wrote anything as deft and telling, or as funny, as the story of the poacher Obey's day in court.

And Hardy would have, must have, relished the old moucher, huddling up to the lime kiln for warmth on a winter's night, moving insensibly closer: "Very early in the morning the quarryman comes to tend his fire, and starts to see on the now redhot and glowing stones, sunk below the rim, the presentment of a skeleton formed of the purest white ashes ..."

The book ends as it begins, with a gun. But the guns were, from the start, only signposts to Eden, and the moment comes at the end of a pheasant prowl: "My finger felt the trigger, and the least increase of pressure would have been fatal; but in the act I hesitated, dropped the barrel, and watched ..."

I have the book still that my cousin lent me. A battered pocket Oxford, 1948. *Paul King* is written in pencil on the flyleaf, the awkward letters falling away down the page, as Paul himself fell one night from an oak tree where pheasants roosted, and broke his back, plying the trade.

ELEANOR WACHTEL

Jigsaw—Sybille Bedford

SYBILLE BEDFORD PUBLISHED HER remarkable autobiographical novel, *Jigsaw*, when she was seventy-eight, a few years before her death. But such are the vagaries of publishing that a book shortlisted for a Booker Prize in 1989 can be a lost classic a decade later.

I first came across her writing some years earlier when I was on holiday in Manzanillo. I had rented a car and, buoyed by that sense of adventure and even mastery that driving a car in a strange country confers, I headed for the small provincial capital of Colima, reputed to be a charming hilltown an easy one hundred kilometers away. Sailing over the crest of a hill, the car lost power, stalled, coasted to a stop in the swampy valley bottom below, and refused to budge. Eventually, I flagged a rickety lemon-yellow bus to the nearest town, Cuyutlan, described in Fodor's Mexico as evocative of an aging Jersey beach resort—in other words, dead. No mechanic.

Four hours later, swarmed by insects, I was sitting on a straight-back kitchen chair in the shade of a gas station, waiting for help from Avis to get back to Manzanillo. But I was rescued first by Bedford's *The Sudden View: A Mexican Journey*, which I had remembered to tuck into my bag that morning. Witty, opinionated and charming, the book had been written in the early 1950s when Bedford had been travelling in Mexico for a year with another writer friend named E., a formidable woman just short of six feet and knowledgeable in history. Two English ladies with husbands somewhere back across the ocean. Thirty years earlier, they were trying to forge a road to the sea through jungle very near where I was now when their car got stuck and they were forced to turn back.

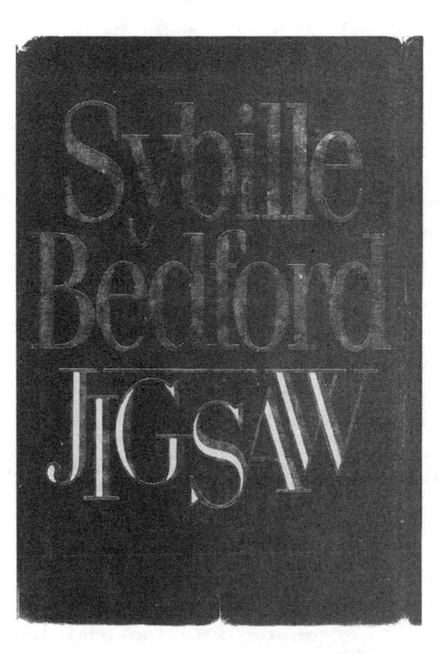

A slightly tattered jacket from the Hamish Hamilton edition, 1989, complete with foil type

Sitting there, absent-mindedly scratching, I was absorbed by her appetite for life, her time in the villa of Don Otavio (the book was later reissued as *A Visit to Don Otavio*), her feeling for "the kind of morning when one cannot bear to be in bed, when one picks up one's tea cup and walks out into the garden. Here the unexpected gift comes every day. Breakfast is laid on the patio: There is fruit, the absurd goldfish are swimming in the fountain and everything smells of geranium; warmth lies gently across one's shoulders; E. has ceased to talk about politics, the housekeeper stops to chat, the boy comes running with hot rolls and butter … it is good to be alive."

It was my first Bedford. It was her first book.

I encountered Bedford's last book in more felicitous circumstances, on vacation again, but this time in France. Installed on a farm in the Alpes-de-Haute-Provence, I read *Jigsaw* in two gulps: a first dense, almost claustrophobic section about her childhood in southern Germany followed by the more sensuous sea, weather and food of France, set not far from where I was staying.

At the beginning of *Jigsaw*, Bedford recounts her earliest memory. She has been left in a pram—though she is over two and well able to walk—in the hallway of her mother's lover's apartment in Copenhagen. It not only (perhaps surprisingly) imbued her with a sympathy for lovers, but was a formative experience somehow perfectly apt for an English writer with such a continental sensibility.

Bedford had an isolated and strange childhood: "I spent the first nine years of my life in Germany, bundled to and fro between two houses. One was outrageously large and ugly; the other was beautiful." So begins *The Legacy*, her 1956 novel, also autobiographical but not quite as transparently as *Jigsaw*, which describes the first twenty or so years of her life. Her parents divorced and she lived in Baden with her father on his country estate, a Schloss that was increasingly impoverished. At one point, she ran away to her sister in Wiesbaden, taking fourth-class trains so she wouldn't be caught (because no one would think to look for her in fourth class). And yes, as she says, "There really was a fourth class in those days," just after World War I.

But most of *Jigsaw* is set in the south of France where she lived with her mother after her father died. And most of the book is about her mother, which is why Bedford calls it "a biographical novel." "One autumn in the late 1920s for no particular reason at all, as it would seem, we began to live in France," she wrote in her 1963 novel, *A Favourite of the Gods*. As Bedford amends in *Jigsaw*, it was in the 1920s and the reason may have been a wise one: her mother and her young Italian lover, Alessandro, were anti-fascists. What was fortuitous was settling in Sanary-sur-Mer, a village along the coast between Toulon and Marseilles. Here Bedford helps look after her mother, who is not only impetuous and seductive, but addicted to gin and morphine. Bedford is too interested in the adult life around her, which came to include Aldous Huxley and his wife, among others, to focus on her own coming-of-age story, which alternates between Sanary and a bedsit in London where she went to study. But she does describe how she almost accidentally loses her virginity, and later develops a crush on an attractive married Frenchwoman.

Bedford writes with the most affable honesty and clarity. I don't know how she does this, but she hits exactly the right tone. You don't have to be eaten by bugs to find her perfectly companionable. Intelligence, resilience and empathy—especially for her doomed mother—inform Bedford's sensibility. She produced not only travel books, a two-volume biography of Aldous Huxley and several novels, but she also reported on trials, lawcourts and judicial procedure, from the obscenity trial of *Lady*

Chatterly's Lover to the murder trial of Jack Ruby and the Auschwitz trials in Frankfurt. Perhaps it's simply her sense of justice and fair play embedded in an appreciation of the complexities and nuances of life. No, it's something more—a generous spirit.

Darren Wershler-Henry

⚜

Treatise on Style—Louis Aragon

"I SHIT ON THE ENTIRE French army." Every time I read that phrase—the very last in Louis Aragon's *Treatise on Style*—it warms the cockles of my black and seedy little heart.

Of course, pretty much everyone has been shitting on the French army since at least the Battle of Agincourt, so the sentiment was not particularly new, even in 1928. But in the context of the *Treatise on Style* (which appeared that year as *Traite du Style*), the aforementioned phrase is merely the last salvo in a book that is the literary equivalent of a hail of razor-blades. Completed in 1927, the *Treatise* was not published until the following year, because literary giants André Gide and Paul Valéry did everything in their power to keep it from going to press.

Louis Aragon, the most elegantly vituperative member of the original Surrealist circle, was for many years André Breton's closest friend and ally; a critic of the Surrealists once wrote that "Aragon's heart beats in Breton's chest." (This trope is particularly apt because the two friends first met during World War I in the French army, where they served as medical officers—Aragon came by his hatred of the army honestly.) Aragon wrote the *Treatise* during an extended stay on the coast of Normandy, while Breton was writing *Nadja*. Even during its inception, the book proved to be an irritant; Aragon hammered out fifteen pages every day to Breton's two or three. After one of the two Surrealists' regular cocktail sessions-cum-workshops, the frustrated Breton remarked to his wife Simone that "what Aragon is writing, which he reads to me nearly every day, is keeping me from writing too much. It's so, so brilliant: you have no idea."

Aragon's caustic Gallicisms are the stuff of which Monty Python routines about apoplectic Frenchmen are made. His own countrymen ("this race of cesspit cleaners"), the American press ("spilled sperm of a continent"), hack writers of all stripes ("subway ink-slingers, fresh-air scribblers, poetypists and anguishographers, high-strung people screaming in the streets while brandishing little pieces of soiled paper, stay-at-home parchment pen pushers, jotters on the run, etc."), Christians ("So many virgins for Lesbos! So many Saint Sebastians for Sodom!"), neo-symbolist poets ("the mussels that attached themselves to the keel of the Drunken Boat"), all are just so many fish in Aragon's barrel. Not even the reader is immune from Aragon's barbs, as this serpentine sentence demonstrates:

> Be aware that if I look both ways before I cross the street—even though not to do so would be more heroic in your eyes and even though you thought you could detect in my writing an idea of existence that is not compatible with prudence—it is because I have no desire to be run over, since I don't believe it is very wise to allow oneself to be run over; this, however, does not take away my right to say that I am not at all grateful to my mother and father for having brought me into the world, and that I also want to arrive on the other side of the street with my right hand—and preferably with my two feet—in order to slap someone more easily, perhaps even you, whom I have the avowed intention of slapping sooner or later.

It is precisely on the level of the sentence that *Style* enters into the fray. As entertaining as the constant stream of invective is, without Aragon's rhetorical gamesmanship—the constant digression and embellishment, the hyperbolic metaphors, the complex punning, the ironic aphorisms, the sudden shifts in tone and diction, the bathetic caricatures, and the all-pervasive *umor* (the Surrealists' term for their own particular strain of sardonic humour)—the *Treatise* would be mere verbal abuse. Rather, the book is a stylistic *tour de force* in the service of a very particular—but still relevant—aesthetic agenda.

After a brief introduction—where Aragon casually mocks the style and accuracy of two brief newspaper articles which describe his arrest for the robbery of several churches—the final section of the *Treatise on Style* presents a table-turning sophistry worthy of Jacques Derrida. It was (and still is) a common misperception that surrealism is a synonym for lazy writing. Instead, Aragon argues, "It is when you write a letter because you have something to say that you are writing any old thing. You give in to your own arbitrariness. But in surrealism all is rigor. Inevitable rigor. The meaning is formed outside of you. The words grouped together mean something in the end, whereas in the other case they meant at the outset what they expressed only later in a very fragmentary way."

Or, as Jack Spicer would write, many years later, "Surrealism is a poem more than this. The intention that things do not fit together. As if my grandmother had chewed on her jigsaw puzzle before she died.... To mess around. To totally destroy the pieces. To build around them."

Edmund White

The Story of Harold—Terry Andrews

This is one of the strangest books I've ever read, probably because it combines elements that have never before or since appeared together. When the book first came out in 1974 it created a minor sensation and then immediately sank out of sight, never to be reprinted, as far as I know. Certainly it is now out of print. "Terry Andrews" is apparently a pen name and though I once heard the real name of the author (someone who in fact was a celebrated children's book writer of the period), I've since forgotten it and I understand he is long since dead.

The novel is recounted by a first-person narrator, named "Terry," who is a New York children's book author who penned an instant classic, *The Story of Harold*, which he reads frequently to a group of kiddies. Harold is a minuscule man who wears a checked vest and a bowler hat, possesses minor magic powers that can change some things but not all, and writes spontaneous poems that sometimes work as spells.

Terry is a hard-drinking, sadistic, death-infatuated bisexual who is a star of the wife-swapping orgy circuit, who has a respectable girlfriend, Anne, and who has two main boyfriends. One is Jim Whittaker, a handsome, cold-hearted egotist, a pushy masochist who drops in on Terry whenever he feels like a roughing up. He's eager to be manhandled and thrashed—but no marks, please, since he must go home to his wife and six children. His children, of course, are all enormous Harold fans, and Terry gets invited to the Whittakers' for Thanksgiving so that he will fill the kids in on still-unpublished episodes in Harold's adventurous life. Harold's biggest admirer is Jim's handsome, blind son, Ben. Although Terry is profoundly in love with Jim, Jim is abundantly clear about his own basic indifference to Terry—a friend, hot sex, nothing more.

Terry's other "slave" is Dan Reilly, a "fire freak" who wants Terry to handcuff him to a stake and burn him alive; in fact, Dan has bought an isolated little house in the suburbs just so this erotic death can be accomplished in privacy. And Dan has carefully constructed his funeral pyre in anticipation of Terry's visit (he's even thoughtfully provided the matches).

That's what I mean by an unusual (unprecedented) combination of elements. The narration, in the form of Terry's diary, alternates among accounts of an evening with Anne at the opera (*Die Frau Ohne Schatten*), a cozy luncheon at the museum between Terry and Jim Whittaker's wife (during which they discuss Jim's human failings), an acrobatic evening with the swingers (the year is 1974, after all), an evening of beating and cigarette burns with Dan Reilly, a hearty, friendly exchange with Terry's loveable cleaning lady ...

Strangest of all are the scenes with Bernard, an impossible, unloveable lump of a little boy whose mother has begged Terry to spend some time with him every so often. Bernard loves only one thing in the world, *The Story of Harold*, and Terry is able to encode life lessons for Bernard in further tales of the tiny figure. Even more bizarrely, Terry talks about the perverted corners of his own nocturnal life in the twee terms of a children's story.

There are faults in this book—it's about fifty pages too long, it has a sentimental ending, the tone seldom strays from an exalted, almost giddy despair. But it is a fearless performance. The narrator's tone (derived, one suspects, from Nabakov's Humbert Humbert) smoothly negotiates its way through all the motley elements. And though "Terry" is a bisexual and a shockingly far-out sadist, nevertheless this novel is the earliest document that renders the feel of Downtown Village gay life in the 1970s—the mix of high culture and perverse sex, the sudden transformation, say, from a night at the opera to an early morning at the baths, the bohemian indifference to bourgeois comfort or even cleanliness, the Sade-like conviction that sexual urges are to be elaborated rather than psychoanalyzed, a complete silence regarding national politics (one would never know this novel was written in the last throes of the Vietnam War), and an enthralled focus on personal destiny. The gym is already a part of the single man's life as is the apartment that is little more than a trick pad. And a life of sex does not in any way preclude a nearly Wagnerian passion (for Jim Whittaker):

> He genuinely loves his wife. At least he must, the amount of sex they make together. He's told me about that, and doesn't lie. (God, I wish that one time he had!) In fact—all you my witnesses—he's described their married life in intimate detail. Among other pleasures on the mental rack, I've been made a confidant ... And he simply adores his kids. I'd like him for that. If there were any seashore left in the storm of emotions I feel for him.

> I'd say I'd "like" him—but the truth within the truth is I love him just for that! The fact that he is an excellent father, a pretty good husband—despite how much he fucks around—those things are what allure me most—they've magnetized me like iron toward his life: the things that make it impossible for me to be anything at all except some casual sex for him ... Terry Andrews—the living dildo, the living whip—that's me!

All the stylistic tricks are here—the voice that interrupts and corrects itself, the demotic-hieratic vocabulary ("fucks around" in the same sentence with "magnetized"), the exclamations as asides in parentheses buried in an otherwise matter-of-fact sentence. This is the voice of the first gay liberation generation: romantic and sexual, unguilty and explicit, nonjudgmental and appreciative, grittily urban and, at the same time, operatic and verging on hysterical self-dramatizing. To me, *The Story of Harold* is a remarkable period piece that reminds us that the 1970s was a period far more sophisticated and humane than our own.

Rudy Wiebe

"The Highwayman"—Alfred Noyes

WITH EIGHT GRADES AND one teacher in a one-room school built of jack-pine in northern Saskatchewan, "memory work," as it was called, was always going on somewhere among the twenty-eight pupils. Often aloud, one child tutoring another, which is how I first heard "The Walrus and the Carpenter" (I knew what those two were—but what was an "oyster"?) and of the mournful Lady of Shalott whose "blood was frozen slowly, / And her eyes were darken'd wholly" as the river carried her to Camelot. Heard, best of all, of the glorious highwayman, a story told by the poet with the silly name, Alfred Noyes—"Racket" we called him. "Stop your Racket!" I was in grade five and the three grade eights were so slow that "The Highwayman" sang completely in my head before they finally mumbled through it. I knew it by heart.

The wind was a torrent of darkness among the gusty trees,

The moon was a ghostly galleon tossed upon cloudy seas,

The road was a ribbon of moonlight over the purple moor,

And the highwayman came riding—

Riding—riding—

The highwayman came riding, up to the old inn door...

At the inn window, Bess, the landlord's black-eyed daughter, is waiting for him:

Plaiting a dark red love-knot into her long black hair.

The highwayman reaches up, promises her a "prize" and:

... "look for me by moonlight,

Watch for me by moonlight,

I'll come to thee by moonlight, though hell should bar the way."

She tumbles the "black cascade" of her perfumed hair down over his breast, he kisses it—"Oh, sweet black waves in the moonlight!"—and gallops away to the west.

But the two are betrayed of course, by Tim, the dumb dog of an ostler to King George's redcoats. Only suspense, and finally death, can follow:

[Bess:]
... her finger moved in the moonlight,
  Her musket shattered the moonlight,
Shattered her breast in the moonlight and warned him—with her death.

[The highwayman:]
... they shot him down on the highway,
  Down like a dog on the highway;
And he lay in his blood on the highway, with the bunch of lace at his throat.

A lost classic? When I started looking, I could find it only in outdated grade-school readers. Alfred Noyes lived until 1958, but his best-known poem was published well before 1913. Is it still available, anywhere, to conjure singing images in some child's head? It would seem Al Purdy remembers "The Highwayman" as irrevocably as I: its rhymes have echoed in his poems for decades, from "Ghengis Khan" (1944) to "Red Fox on Highway 500" (1981); perhaps it is inevitable that this English heritage of legendary romance affects all my generation's Canadian education.

Crown 8vo. 7s. 6d. net.

Ballads & Poems

By ALFRED NOYES

THIS is the first selection in one volume of poems from all of the author's former books, with many poems hitherto unpublished. It ranges from early ballads like "The Highwayman" (described by a famous critic as the best narrative poem in existence for oral delivery) to the elfin epic of "The Forest of Wild Thyme" (which must be read

The front cover of a promotional insert from Alfred Noyes's Ballads and Poems, *published by William Blackwood & Sons, Edinburgh, 1928*

But perhaps the poem most strongly evokes "lost classic" for me because in 1944-45, when I subliminally learned it, my black-haired sister Helen, barely seventeen, lay in our farm home wasting into a shadow because of an enlarged heart brought on by rheumatic fever caught years before, they said, at the school Christmas concert while she ran back and forth from the teacherage in the fierce cold clothed in nothing but a dancing fairy costume of pink crêpe paper. All that last winter she dreamed of a boy barely two miles away who, of course, manly as he was becoming, never visited her, but her closest friend, Isola, came frequently riding a huge, furry ploughhorse that snorted great clouds into the stunning air. Isola loved "The Highwayman" too, and she and I would play it back and forth, line by line between us, while Helen checked us in the reader. When Helen died in late March, Isola brought her own new dress, which she had never yet worn, for Helen to be buried in. I remember my sister in the coffin, her gentle face so devastated, her glorious black hair and the shining dress, a wide white bow tied at her chin. And her emaciated arms under crêpe paper flowers crossed below her breast.

At age ten I knew nothing about "many-tower'd Camelot" or velvet coats or ostlers or love-knots or moors; I had never tasted an oyster, nor seen a sea. But I knew the distant "tlot—tlot, tlot—tlot" of hoofbeats approaching at night, and also, as it sailed through the sky, "the ghostly galleon" of the moon; above the silver green or the spare winter crowns of aspen I had seen that, seen it often.

C. K. Williams

Smut

IT HAD NO TITLE, and, as far as I ever knew, no author. As it came into my hand, there was no title page; it was a carbon, on quarter sheets of onion-skin paper, stapled together: the original had been typed, that meant by hand, word by word, letter by letter. I suppose it would have been soiled, worn, but I only remember now the sheer miraculousness of it, of its existence, and even more of its having found me.

It's hard to believe how efficient the system of sexual obliteration actually was in those days; this would be the late 1940s. At least as far as I was concerned—I was twelve, living at the edge of a small city—the whole realm of the sexual was something that happened entirely within me, in my body in shame and delight, and in my consciousness in blind secrecy, and an absolute, all but ascetic isolation.

There was this thing, about which one inferred auras from comments adults would infrequently mumble to each other; this looming, inchoate alp of experience which evoked among one's classmates a unique kind of inexplicable, supercilious laughter, and this other thing one felt, not felt really, was taken by, wrenched, colonized by, awake and in sleep, in thought and whatever it is at that age that lurks beneath thought, perhaps in what comes to be what we call "fantasy," but isn't that yet, because there are no narratives yet with which to embody it.

My best friend was two years older than I was; he knew remarkably more about the world than I did and it was he to whom the work had been vouchsafed. I was sleeping over at his house, he must have said, "Look at this," and there it was: from the first half page I knew exactly what it was, knew how much, violently, without knowing I had, needed it, for so many now immediately self-evident reasons.

Here is the book: two women meet, and are astonished to realize that they are perfect duplicates of one another, same features, same hair, exactly the same figure. (One, later in the story, will turn out to have a mole, on the underside—the underside! amazing—of one breast, which ultimately will add welcome complexities to their adventures.) Their names are Ruth and Louise. They go to one of their homes, undress, examine each other, caress one another, very complicatedly, even poignantly, it seems to me now, and soon conspire to change places in their lives. Both of these secret sharers is married; one, as I recall, has a lover.

The story evolves: I really can't recall a single word of it, because it doesn't come to me word by word; I don't know if it's the kind of crude pornography that will be mass-produced in the sixties and seventies when the censorship laws have been loosened, or if it's a less vulgar Victorian excretion. Is any of that really less vulgar? That's not the point: none of anything like that matters at all; it was the reading of those marvellously semi-translucent pages that remains so preciously vivid.

Nostalgically, I can think of the innocent I was and of how many complexities of sexual mechanics were explicated by the text, but even that seems incidental. What still sears is the way the words came into me, with such astonishing force. As I remember it, I had nothing but the most blurred, uncertain image of anything actual; I suppose more precise images must have flowed, but they seemed to come after the words: the words were being etched, chiselled, into my—what? My mind, my brain, my emotions?

No, something previous to all that; there was some bond that seemed to be being forged between the very core of my corporeal and intellectual existence and the act of taking experience into myself through the word. The sensuousness of the event, and there was so much, it seems, at least now—I can't care any more what it was then—to have been divided between the erotics it flamingly evoked, and my absorption of them. It was as though, as poets say, I wasn't reading, but being read.

Of course poetry has to come into it somewhere, because poetry, too, seems now to have always been there. Perhaps it was poetry, then, which existed previous to the rest; that indelible attachment to the double existence of life and art, and art in life.

Michael Winter

N by E—Rockwell Kent

Thoreau once said that he could not read far in a good book but he must lay it down and take up living. And this is precisely the agenda behind Rockwell Kent's *N by E*: a blend of the physical and spiritual, part text, part picture book.

Written in 1930, you must get the original edition. The reprint in the seventies is a mere photocopy on thinner paper. It loses the impact of first impression. Most of that reprint was remaindered and stored in a shed, which suffered smoke and water damage in a fire. The entire second edition has a kippered scent to it.

I suggest you memorize the shape and colour of the book, and find a 1930 first edition sandwiched within a wall of travel memoirs. This is how I found mine in a Toronto bookstore.

It's a book I love to read at random. Kent's hand is all over the design. There is the surprise of the woodcuts. Juicy black images, highly stylized, of squares of land and sky, aerial views of coastline, moody Atlantic landscapes, an oarsman straining to row a punt, men in a cutter struggling with sheets, romantic night visions in dramatic chiaroscuro of bowsprits and figureheads, and naked men linked to masts and spars in some sensuous crucifixion, all stamped into the book by something heavy and convinced. Each woodcut a deep, decisive black pool of ink printed on pages thick as the skin of a labourer. It's enough to make anyone pick up a set of carving tools and try a block of maple.

N by E chronicles Kent's voyage to Greenland in 1929, aboard the thirty-three-foot *Direction*. The cutter sails into the port city of St. John's, which gives Kent the chance to discuss the time he lived in Brigus, Newfoundland, back in 1914. The Brigus chapter is my favourite.

Kent had great hopes for his life in Newfoundland. He planned to stay for the long haul. The Brigus flashback begins with a dark, hopeful woodcut of the town and a man strolling along a tongue of land towards it. The man is Kent, and he is walking away from his house, the oldest wooden house in Newfoundland, built by the Pomeroys in 1786. That house still stands (sheathed in cedar shingles), and I have walked there, past the chuckling brook, the dandelions and oak, the big birch tree, paced off his house (forty-five feet long, fourteen wide). I have taken a sprig from a crab-apple and replanted it in my own garden.

Kent sent for his wife and children. His letters to friends are full of promise. Kent's anticipation of his existence in Newfoundland coloured the rest of his life. Over the next eighteen months, his hopes would erode, as he suffered the gossip of outport Newfoundland.

The First World War had begun, and people remembered how Kent had sung German lieder at church, how he'd ordered ten tons of coal for the winter, how no one was allowed into his artist's space, how he'd demanded that a mysterious tool chest of his, which had sunk to the bottom of Halifax harbour, be salvaged and sent to him, how he could be found rambling over the hills, making sketches of the coastline.

It was rumoured he was a German spy, supplying fuel to a submarine and mailing war maps disguised as paintings. These rumours reached the authorities in St. John's.

Kent did nothing to alleviate these rumours, in fact he defiantly encouraged them. He painted a German eagle on the door to his studio, and wrote "Bomb Shop" beneath it. He sent letters to the papers saying he hoped the German navy would obliterate Newfoundland. While passing a prisoner-of-war camp in Carbonear, he shouted, in German, that the Kaiser was winning the war.

After a year of gossip and correspondence with the government, the Kent family was ordered to leave the colony. Bitter but relieved by the decree, Kent packed up his family and returned to New York. But Kent wasn't a German spy. He was an outsider for sure, an individualist, an artist who appreciated German culture, a socialist, an explorer and a romantic figure. All this is exposed in *N by E*, a quiet, almost forgotten book, a communique of an uncompromising creative spirit struggling to express itself.

Kent alludes to the failure in Newfoundland early on in *N by E*. Even so, he still holds a deep affection for the land and people. He still nurtures the promise he'd expected Newfoundland to offer. He spent the rest of his life travelling to the globe's extremes, to Greenland, Alaska and Tierra del Fuego. Another thirty-eight years and two wives would slip by before Kent's final experience with Newfoundland would occur.

In 1968, then-premier Joey Smallwood discovered the fifty-three-year-old correspondence between Kent and the Newfoundland government. Smallwood was alarmed at the treatment Kent had received.

He invited the artist to return to Newfoundland. Kent, still robust at eighty-six, accepted. He returned to Brigus and walked towards the house along that black tongue of land he had carved on a block of wood half a century before. That woodcut, contained on page sixty-six of *N by E*, captures a time prior to the acceptance of a doomed venture. The moment of ecstatic bliss at being alive in the world.

N by E chronicles Kent's adventures in Greenland and yet I have a sense that had things gone differently in Brigus, it might have been a book about his life in Newfoundland. *N by E* captures more than the story it intended to tell when it was published. It contains, seventy years later, the story of an artist who was not fully understood or accepted, in the time and places in which he lived.

RONALD WRIGHT

Pincher Martin—William Golding

> Think about women then or eating. Think about eating women, eating men, crunching up Alfred, that other girl, that boy … lie restful as a log and consider the gnawed tunnel of life right up to this uneasy intermission.
>
> This rock.

WILLIAM GOLDING'S *PINCHER MARTIN* was one of the first grown-up novels I read, somewhere in my early teens when I was still looking for sea stories, unaware till then that my taste for salty melodrama had begun to cloy and it was time to move on. I probably read half the book—as anyone can—thinking it was indeed about a torpedoed sailor struggling to survive on a bare rock in the North Atlantic. Yet its startling imagery and metaphysical freight must have sunk in, because a few years later, while experimenting with hallucinogenic mushrooms in the mountains of Oaxaca, I saw my hands turn into lobster claws—the claws of Pincher Martin as he dies.

Lieutenant Christopher Martin, an actor before he is called up for convoy duty in World War II, has always "pinched" things not on offer—a friend's wife, a girl's virginity, countless cruel and shabby victories over friends. He plays foul because winning is the thing that matters and the only alternative he can imagine is to be devoured. He knows himself for a cannibal: "You could eat with your cock or with your fist, or with your voice."

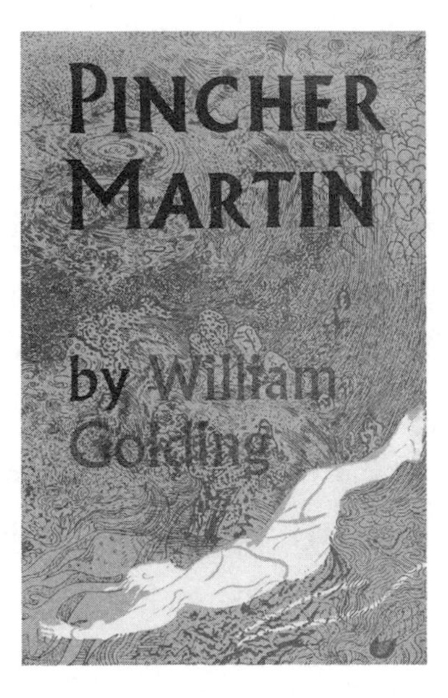

The 1956 Faber & Faber jacket

Contemplating murder at the moment a U-boat strikes, he is blown from ship to sea, the eater suddenly eaten. He washes up on an uncharted rock, where he fights cold, hunger, thirst and voracious gulls like "flying reptiles." But Pincher's struggle is not really with external Nature; it's with human nature and his own nature, the "dark centre" he has become in life. There are echoes of Pedro Serrano ("There is someone else on the rock with me. He crept out and slugged me"), of Caliban and Crusoe ("I will tie it down with names").

Pincher is "a good hater," and his reward is a nightmare built of the memories strewn in the wake of his ruthless life. Slowly and inexorably, as he writhes on the rock, the poison seeps from sealed chambers of his past into the welter (a favourite word here) of his mind. There are obvious religious themes: that we make our own heavens and hells; that hell is listening forever to one's own monologue; that whether or not one believes in an afterlife, the moment of death viewed from inside may well be everlasting. Golding underlines all this in a shock ending that a lesser writer could never have got away with. But the book transcends belief to examine conscience and consciousness; remembrance and destiny; the rise of our personality and our species; and the forces inside ourselves that we have every reason to fear, for behind us are a million years of ruthless victories.

I reread *Pincher Martin* at twenty, soon after the Oaxaca trip, and then not again until I bought a copy recently. I think it was out of print until Golding won the Nobel prize; even now it's hard to find, squeezed out by *Lord of the Flies*. I worried that it might have palled like other adolescent tastes—sweet Vermouth, white lipstick (on girls), magic mushrooms. But on every reading I've found more to admire and think about, more phrases and thoughts to cheer. Few writers have attempted half his themes in twice the room, barely two hundred pages of jaggedly poetic prose. Each reading cuts deeper as one reads further and further beneath the dying seaman, nearer to one's own being, and then beyond self to considerations of what it is to be human, in both the evolutionary and moral sense.

> I will tell you what a man is.... He is a freak, an ejected foetus robbed of his natural development, thrown out in the world with a naked covering of parchment, with too little room for his teeth and a soft bulging skull like a bubble. But nature stirs a pudding there and sets a thunderstorm flickering inside the hardening globe....

Afterword

JAVIER MARÍAS

Imaginative Wickedness

DURING A RECENT TRIP to Buenos Aires, a city I was visiting for the first time, I rediscovered a type of dealer in old books whom I thought had disappeared from the face of the earth, except, perhaps, from England, where everything seems to persist in its original or Dickensian state. I mean the type of book dealer who knows absolutely nothing about what he stocks and sells, and therefore doesn't usually mark his books with prices, but decides how much to charge on the spot after hearing the prospective buyer's query, and particularly the tone in which it is made. Such a dealer is guided less by the binding, the print run, the date of the edition or the author than by the interest betrayed in the customer's way of looking at and handling a particular volume. These are people who have been seasoned or, rather, trained by years of experience watching their customers browse. For these men, we buyers must, I suppose, be an open book; our reaction tells them much more about the tome in our hands than that tome could have told them when it was resting on its shelf a minute before. They know nothing about their wares but they do know how to drill into the human psyche; they've learned to interpret the slight trembling of fingers that go to the spine of a book, the momentary blinking of someone who can't believe his eyes are seeing the title they've sought for years; they know how to perceive the speed with which you seize this long-wanted but unfindable book, as if—and although you're alone in the bookshop—you were afraid the swifter glove of another hunter might appear precisely at that moment and snatch it from you. In the presence of one of these disciples of Sherlock Holmes, you feel as closely observed as an inmate in a prison yard who knows the guard is scrutinizing his every movement and gesture. In the presence of such a book dealer you must rediscover, in self-defense and in defense of your wallet, the art of dissimulation: you must control your emotion, your impatience, your agitation and your joy, making, instead, a show of disinterest in or even disdain for the thing you most covet; you must count to ten before taking down from the shelf the volume your eyes have fastened on in disbelief and greed.

The truth is that book dealing has changed a great deal in the last fifteen years, especially in Spain, where not only has the intuitive and waylaying type of dealer I rediscovered in Buenos Aires ceased to exist, but the fair, just and understanding dealer as well. The increasingly scant pickings (there has been a certain vogue for this sort of thing, and we're in a period when readers buy for their libraries but rarely sell from them) has inflated prices to an absurd degree, and the few individuals who remain dedicated to this hodgepodge of a trade have done their research and are equipped with computerized catalogues that instantly let them know the highest possible price they can demand for something they generally acquired for a quarter of the sum, or maybe less. Nothing against that, but the *aficionado* of this type of hunt has forever lost the element of chance that once made itself felt as he entered one of those dusty enclaves, apparently forgotten by human eyes, which nowadays have little tolerance for shadows.

The feeling of loss has less to do with the impossibility of finding something of value for a modest price than with the growing improbability of meeting any odd or adventuresome people at the helms of such establishments. The contemporary book dealer is an efficient, well-informed man, much like the manager of the book section of a chain of large department stores; the difference between them is that the latter will consult the book-review sections of newspapers and the lists of bestsellers while the former will turn to more recondite or arcane catalogues. But both will undoubtedly limit themselves to making a few taps on a keyboard.

In this day and age, it isn't easy to find the kind of hallucinatory characters I met a few years ago in England. One of my biggest surprises came when I entered a dimly lit bookshop and saw, sitting at his table with his hands crossed, a middle-aged individual wearing the black and white garb of the Dominican order (or is it the Benedictine? I'm not well versed in such matters). I immediately thought I had blundered into a religious bookstore and was about to leave when, in a kindly voice, the man asked me what my interests were. I just wanted to have a look around, I said, and he invited me to do so with a reverential flourish of his arm. If the shop specialized in anything, it wasn't religion but tales and novels of terror. When I inquired as to the reason for this focus, he gave me the following explanation: the place belonged to his niece, and was primarily stocked with books that the brothers of his monastery, located on the outskirts of Lymington, bought, read and then immediately got rid of, since it wasn't considered proper for them to accumulate too many belongings. Once the books had been used, they sold them so they could acquire new ones, which they never kept for very long. When I commented that this didn't exactly answer my question, the Dominican raised his hands to his bald pate in a very theatrical way—it was almost the flamboyant gesture of an extravagant homosexual—and shouted, "But of course, you're a foreigner; how could you be expected to know anything about the tastes of the English clergy!" He then explained that the genre of terror was the preferred reading matter of British priests and monks—"with exceptions," he cautioned—regardless of the church or order to which they belonged, and that many of them had also made marvellous contributions to the genre (he mentioned Malden and Summers). "For a priest," he said, "the best way to be close to God is to be close to Evil, close to the Enemy. All there is to know about God can be learned very quickly, a few years of studying theology are really enough. Goodness is equal to itself, it has no disguises and precisely because it is goodness there is no deceit in its bosom, no duplicity, no subterfuge. It is immutable and very simple, and therefore it is easy to know and easy to threaten. In order to defend it, one must study the character, wiles and imagination of what threatens it: wickedness is imaginative. We lead such a cloistered life that we have little opportunity to come into contact with that, with things that are wicked and imaginative, and so we come to know them in the books produced by the most twisted minds and the most venomous pens. Anyway," he added, "what we love best always bores us."

Even as I left that shop, with two or three fairly significant acquisitions, I was still wondering if the whole thing hadn't been staged and my interlocutor a gay man who took perverse pleasure in dressing up as a Dominican. When I got home and looked over the books again at greater length I noticed, however, that two of them bore the names of their former owners on the first page, and in both cases the names were preceded by the word Father.

ON ANOTHER OCCASION, I met a man who presided over a bookshop that had more rare and select titles than almost any other I had ever been in: first editions of works by Joyce, Dickens and Jane Austen, and by Conrad, some of them signed and dedicated by the authors, and also extreme rarities such as—I remember—the only four books ever published by the mysterious and outlandish Count Stenbock, who succeeded in scandalizing Oscar Wilde. Items like these had to be extremely costly, and were undoubtedly not within my means. Even so, partly out of curiosity and partly to try my luck, I asked how much one of them was. After removing the book from my hands, looking it over carefully and explaining the exceptional characteristics of that particular edition, the dealer's response was, "This volume is not for sale." I scanned the shop a little longer, then asked about another book, and the process was repeated; the man—a polished, almost elegant man—took it from me, stroked it, sang its praises and concluded, "It's not for sale." And the same thing happened with every volume that attracted my interest, so that, although a certain type of reaction can seem rude in England, at the fifth attempt I couldn't contain myself and asked him, ill-humoredly, "Why don't you just tell me which ones are for sale and we can speed things up a little?" The man stiffened with what seemed to be slightly wounded professionalism. He grabbed away the last I book I had taken down, blew off some nonexistent dust (in fact there was no dust in that bookshop, which is unheard-of) and answered haughtily, "Oh, most of them are, most of them are, what do you think? I'm not about to work against the interests of my own business." In light of this response, I inquired about two or three more titles, but always with the same degree of success. "This certainly isn't your lucky day," he said; "*that's* not for sale either." I later learned from one of my colleagues at Oxford that the man was indeed working against the interests of his own business, or, rather, that despite the fact that his shop opened onto the street and there was a sign on the door saying *Open* or *Closed* depending on the time of day, he had no business. He was a collector so fanatical, so proud of his possessions, that after having amassed one of the best libraries in the country, he found it unbearable that no one, or only the few acquaintances who came to visit him, ever saw or admired it. So he decided to pass himself off as a book dealer in order to enjoy the astonishment and greed that his exquisite treasures inspired in incautious passers-by or aspiring clients. Small wonder that nothing was ever for sale.

These original and unrepeatable characters are disappearing even in the country of Dickens, which is less and less Dickensian. To go into a rare bookshop now is more a transaction than an adventure. But at least I had the good fortune, not long ago—and even if it was on the other side of the Atlantic—of feeling the (already anachronistic) emotion of someone who notices that his states of mind are being interpreted and shivers to feel himself sized up by keen, wary and expert eyes, eyes that may be well acquainted with the imaginative capacities of wickedness.

—translated by Esther Allen

Notes on Contributors

MARGARET ATWOOD is the author of more than twenty-five books of poetry, fiction and non-fiction. Her most recent novel is *The Blind Assassin*. She lives in Toronto.

MURRAY BAIL lives in Sydney, Australia. His novel *Eucalyptus* won the 1999 Commonwealth Writers Prize for Best Book.

RUSSELL BANKS's most recent work is a collection of stories called *The Angel on the Roof*. His many novels include *Cloudsplitter* and *The Sweet Hereafter*, which was made into a feature film directed by Atom Egoyan. He lives in upstate New York.

CHRISTIAN BÖK is the author of *Crystallography: Book I of Information Theory*, a pataphysical encyclopedia, nominated in 1994 for the Gerald Lampert Memorial Award. Bök is currently completing work on a univocal lipogram, entitled *Eunoia*. He lives in Toronto.

ROO BORSON has published ten books of poetry, the most recent being *Introduction to the Introduction to Wang Wei*, a collaborative work by Pain Not Bread (Roo Borson, Kim Maltman, Andy Patton). Also an occasional essayist, she lives in Toronto.

ROBERT BOYERS is editor of the quarterly *Salmagundi*, Tisch Professor of Arts and Letters at Skidmore College (Saratoga Springs, New York) and Director of the New York State Summer Writers Institute. He is the author of six critical books, and reviews books frequently for *The New Republic*.

BRIAN BRETT is the author of many books, of which the most recent are *Poems: New and Selected, Allegories of Love and Disaster* and *The Colour of Bones in a Stream*. He has just completed his latest novel, *Coyote Sunset*. He lives on a farm on Salt Spring Island.

NATALEE CAPLE is the author of one novel, *The Plight of Happy People in an Ordinary World*; one short-story collection, *The Heart Is Its Own Reason*; and one book of poetry, *A More Tender Ocean*. She lives in Toronto.

ANNE CARSON lives in Canada.

GEORGE ELLIOTT CLARKE is an Africadian (African-Canadian) poet, playwright, librettist and screenwriter. His latest works include *Beatrice Chancy*, which is both a play and an opera, and *Gold Indigoes*, a chapbook of American lyrics.

KAREN CONNELLY is the author of several books of poetry and non-fiction. She is the recipient of the Pat Lowther Award for poetry and the Governor General's Award for Non-fiction. Her most recent book of poetry is *The Border Surrounds Us*. She is currently writing her first novel, *The Lizard Cage*.

CAROLE CORBEIL is a novelist and arts journalist born in Montreal and now living in Toronto. Also the author of *Voice-over*, her most recent book is *In The Wings*, published in 1998.

ROBERT CREELEY edited the renowned *Black Mountain Review* years ago for the college of that name in North Carolina. He was New York State Poet (1989–91), a proud feat for a New Englander and even more so for one who has spent his last thirty-three years more or less in Buffalo. His recent books are *Life & Death, So There* and *Day Book of a Virtual Poet.*

SARAH ELLIS never grew out of reading children's books. With luck and guile she managed to turn this guilty secret into a patchwork career involving fiction writing, reviewing, lecturing, storytelling and working as a librarian—all with an emphasis on children's literature. Her latest book is *From Reader to Writer: Teaching Writing Through Classic Children's Books.*

JEFFREY EUGENIDES is the author of the novel *The Virgin Suicides.* He is currently a Fellow at the American Academy in Berlin.

DOUGLAS FETHERLING works in Toronto as a poet, fiction writer, teacher and small-press publisher. His latest book is *Madagascar: Poems & Translations.*

CHARLES FORAN is the author of five books, including *Butterfly Lovers* and *The Story of My Life (So Far)*. An award-winning writer, journalist and broadcaster who lived in China for three years, he now lives in Peterborough.

HELEN GARNER is an Australian whose published work includes novels, short stories, journalism and non-fiction. Her most recent books are *The First Stone*, a best-selling account of a university sexual harassment case, and *True Stories*, her selected journalism. She lives in Melbourne.

WAYNE GRADY is a writer and translator living in the country north of Kingston, Ontario. Also the author of *The Dinosaur Project* and *The Quiet Limit of the World*, his most recent book is *The Bone Museum: Travels in the Lost Worlds of Dinosaurs and Birds.*

GITHA HARIHARAN's first novel, *The Thousand Faces of Night*, was published in 1992 and won the Commonwealth Writers Prize for Best First Book. She has also published a collection of short stories, *The Art of Dying*, and a novel, *The Ghosts of Vasu Master*. Her most recent novel, *When Dreams Travel*, was published in 1999.

DIANA HARTOG has published three award-winning books of poetry—*Matinee Light, Candy from Strangers* and *Polite to Bees*—and most recently a novel, *The Photographer's Sweethearts*.

STEVEN HEIGHTON is an award-winning poet and fiction writer. His first novel, *The Shadow Boxer*, was published in 2000. Among his other books are *Flight Paths of the Emperor, On earth as it is* and *The Ecstasy of Skeptics*. He lives in Kingston, Ontario.

MICHAEL HELM's novel *The Projectionist* was published in 1997, and was a finalist for the Giller Prize.

GREG HOLLINGSHEAD's recent books are *The Healer*, a novel, and the short-story collection *The Roaring Girl*, which won the Governor General's Award for Fiction. He lives in Edmonton.

ANNE HOLZMAN is a freelance writer and a student in the Master of Fine Arts in Writing program at Hamline University in St. Paul, Minnesota.

ISABEL HUGGAN is the author of two collections of short stories, *The Elizabeth Stories* and *You Never Know*. She was born in Kitchener, Ontario, but now lives in France, and is working on her third collection.

LAIRD HUNT is the author of *Dear Sweetheart* and the forthcoming short novel *The Paris Stories (small sicknesses of love)*. He lives in New York City.

NANCY HUSTON writes both in French and English. Among her novels are *Histoire d'Omaya*, *The Goldberg Variations* and *The Mark of the Angel*. She lives in Paris.

SIRI HUSTVEDT is a novelist, most recently of *The Enchantment of Lily Dahl* and *The Blindfold*. She is also the author of *Yonder*, a collection of essays. She lives in New York.

JOHN WINSLOW IRVING was born in Exeter, New Hampshire, in 1942. He is the author of the Oscar-winning screenplay for *The Cider House Rules* and nine novels, among them *A Widow for One Year, The Hotel New Hampshire, The World According to Garp, A Prayer for Owen Meany* and *A Son of the Circus*. He lives in Toronto and southern Vermont.

PICO IYER is the author of six books, most recently *The Global Soul: Jet Lag, Shopping Malls, and the Search for Home*, a collection of essays called *Tropical Classical*, and *Cuba and the Night*, a novel. He lives in Japan and California.

GORDON JOHNSTON was born and raised in Thunder Bay on the north shore of Lake Superior. He studied at the University of Toronto and Harvard, and has taught Canadian Poetry and Native Studies at Trent University in Peterborough, Ontario for twenty-eight years. His novel, *Inscription Rock*, was published in 1981.

WAYNE JOHNSTON was born and raised in Newfoundland and now lives in Toronto. Among his recent works are *The Colony of Unrequited Dreams* and *Baltimore's Mansion*, which won the inaugural Charles Taylor Prize for Literary Non-fiction. His 1994 novel, *Human Amusements,* is about to be made into a feature film, as was his earlier novel, *The Divine Ryans.*

JANICE KULYK KEEFER lives in Toronto. Her latest books are *Marrying the Sea*, which won the CAA Best Book of Poetry for 1998, and *Honey and Ashes, a Story of Family.*

WENDY LESSER, the founding editor of *The Threepenny Review*, is the author of *The Amateur: An Independent Life of Letters, His Other Half: Men Looking at Women Through Art* and *Pictures at an Execution.* She has won prizes and fellowships from the Guggenheim Foundation, the National Endowment for the Humanities and the American Academy of Arts and Letters, among others. She lives in Berkeley, California.

PHILIP LEVINE is the author of more than ten collections of poetry, including *They Feed They Lion*, *The Mercy* and the Pulitzer Prize-winning *Simple Truth.* He lives in Fresno, California.

ALAN LIGHTMAN is a novelist, essayist, physicist, and educator currently a professor of humanities and senior lecturer in physics at the Massachusetts Institute of Technology (MIT). He is a fellow of the American Academy of Arts and Sciences and the recipient of the American Institute of Physics Andrew Gemant Award for linking science to the humanities. His novels include *The Diagnosis, Einstein's Dreams* and *Good Benito.*

DEREK LUNDY trained as a lawyer but makes his living as a writer. He is the author of *Godforsaken Sea: Racing the World's Most Dangerous Waters*, and *Scott Turow: Meeting the Enemy*. He lives in Toronto, where he is writing a book about a square-rigger voyage round Cape Horn.

DAVID MALOUF is the author of ten novels, including *Remembering Babylon*, which was a finalist for the Booker Prize in 1993 and *The Conversations at Curlow Creek*. His latest book is *Dream Stuff*, a collection of short fiction. Malouf lives in Sydney.

JAVIER MARÍAS' colletcion of short stories, *When I Was Mortal*, was just published in English by New Directions. His books have been translated into twenty-two languages. Marías lives in Madrid.

HARRY MATHEWS is the author, most recently, of *The Journalist*, which won the Americas Award in Literature for the best work of fiction. He is a novelist, poet and essayist, and divides his time between New York and Paris.

W. S. MERWIN is the author of over twelve collections of poetry, the most recent of which are *The Folding Cliffs, The River Sound, East Window*, a collection of Asian translations, and *Purgatorio*, a translation of the central section of Dante's *Divine Comedy*. He lives in Hawaii.

ANCHEE MIN's most recent novel is *Becoming Madame Mao*. She is also the author of *Red Azalea: A True Story of Life and Love in China* and of *Katherine*, a novel. She lives in California.

JIM MOORE lives in St. Paul, Minnesota. His most recent book of poems is *The Long Experience of Love*. He is currently finishing a new collection of poems.

ERIN MOURÉ's most recent books of poetry are *A Frame of the Book* (also called *The Frame of a Book*), *Search Procedures* and *Pillage Laud*. She lives in Montreal, where she works as a translator.

SUSAN MUSGRAVE's most recent book of poetry is *What the Small Day Cannot Hold: Collected Poems 1970–1985*. She has just published her third novel, *Cargo of Orchids*.

MICHAEL ONDAATJE was born in Sri Lanka and moved to Canada in 1962. He is the author of *The English Patient* (for which he received both the Governor General's Award for Fiction and the Booker Prize), *In the Skin of a Lion, Coming Through Slaughter, The Collected Works of Billy the Kid* and, most recently, *Anil's Ghost*. He is also the author of a memoir and several collections of poetry, the latest being *Handwriting*. He lives in Toronto and is a contributing editor to *Brick* magazine.

CARYL PHILLIPS was born in St. Kitts, grew up in England, and now divides his time between New York and London. He is the author of six novels, most recently *The Nature of Blood*, and two works of non-fiction, including *The European Tribe*. His awards include the Martin Luther King Memorial Prize, fellowships from the Guggenheim and Lannan Foundations and the James Tait Black Memorial Prize.

CASSANDRA PYBUS is one of Australia's most admired non-fiction writers. Her latest book, *The Devil and James McAuley*, won the National Non-fiction Award at the 2000 Adelaide Festival. Her previous books include *Community of Thieves* and *The White Rajas of Sarawak.*

ANDREW PYPER is the author of the novel *Lost Girls*, as well as *Kiss Me*, a collection of short stories. He lives in Toronto.

MICHAEL REDHILL lives and works in Toronto, where he is the managing editor of *Brick*. His first novel, *Martin Sloane*, will be published in 2001, as will his fifth collection of poetry, *Light-crossing*.

BILL RICHARDSON is a bestselling writer and broadcaster, currently the host of "Richardson's Roundup" on CBC Radio One. His books include *Scorned & Beloved: Dead of Winter Meetings with Canadian Eccentrics*, *The Bachelor Brothers' Bed & Breakfast* and, most recently, *After Hamelin*, his first book for children.

EDEN ROBINSON is a Haisla/Heiltsuk writer, the author of *Monkey Beach*, a coming-of-age novel set in Kitamaat, B.C., and *Traplines*, a collection of short stories. She was recently Writer-in-Residence at the Whitehorse Public Library in Whitehorse, Yukon Territory.

LEON ROOKE's latest novel is *The Fall of Gravity*. His other novels include *Fat Woman* and *Shakespeare's Dog*, for which he won a Governor General's Award, and *A Good Baby*, which was recently made into a feature film.

JANE RULE was born in New Jersey in 1931 and has lived on Canada's west coast since 1956. She is the author of many books, most recently *After the Fire* and *Memory Board*, as well as the classic lesbian novel *Desert of the Heart*, the basis for the movie *Desert Hearts*.

JOANNA SCOTT is the author of five novels, including *Make Believe, The Manikin* and *Arrogance*, and a collection of stories, *Various Antidotes*. She lives in Rochester, NY.

SARAH SHEARD is a fiction writer living in Toronto. Her third novel, *The Hypnotist*, was preceded by *Almost Japanese* and *The Swing Era*.

ELENI SIKELIANOS is the author of *to speak while dreaming*, *The Lover's Numbers* and *The Book of Tendons*. Forthcoming is *Blue Guide* and *Of Sun, Of History, Of Seeing*. She has been conferred a National Endowment for the Arts Fellowship in poetry, the James D. Phelan Award for California-born writers, and several Gertrude Stein Awards for Innovative North American Writing. Though she makes her home in New York, she is currently working on a writing project as a Fulbright Fellow in Greece.

SAM SOLECKI is Professor of English at the University of Toronto. He is a former editor of *The Canadian Forum*, and his most recent book is *The Last Canadian Poet: An Essay on Al Purdy*.

ESTA SPALDING is a poet, most recently of *Lost August*. She lives in Vancouver where she writes for film and television, and is a contributing editor to *Brick*.

LINDA SPALDING is the editor and publisher of *Brick*, as well as the author of the novels *Daughters of Captain Cook*, *The Paper Wife* and the forthcoming *Mere*, co-written with Esta Spalding. Her most recent book is *The Follow*, a work of non-fiction.

LAWRENCE SUTIN is the author of *Divine Invasions: A Life of Philip K. Dick*; *Jack and Rochelle: A Holocaust Story of Love and Resistance*; and two recently published books, *A Postcard Memoir* and *Do What Thou Wilt: A Life of Aleister Crowley.*

SHARON THESEN's latest collection of poetry is *A Pair of Scissors.* Also recently published are *Charles Olson and Frances Boldereff: A Modern Correspondence* (co-edited with Ralph Maud), and *News & Smoke*, a volume of Thesen's selected poems, which came out in 1999.

COLM TOIBIN was born in Ireland in 1955 and lives in Dublin. His four novels include *The Heather Blazing* (1992) and T*he Blackwater Lightship*, which was short-listed for the Booker Prize in 1999.

LOLA LEMIRE TOSTEVIN has published five collections of poetry, one collection of essays and a novel, *Frog Moon*. Her second novel, *The Jasmine Man*, is forthcoming. She lives in Toronto with her family.

MICHAEL TURNER's books include *Company Town*, *Hard Core Logo*, *American Whiskey Bar* and, most recently, *The Pornographer's Poem*. He lives in Vancouver.

SEÁN VIRGO was born in Malta in 1940, raised in South Africa, Ireland and the UK, and has been living in Canada for over thirty years. He has published four books of poetry to date, four works of short fiction and one novel, *Selakhi*. He currently lives in southern Saskatchewan.

ELEANOR WACHTEL is a journalist and broadcaster. She has been the host of CBC Radio's "Writers & Company" since its inception in 1990. Two selections of her interviews have been published: *Writers & Company* and *More Writers & Company*. She is also the host of CBC Radio's "The Arts Today" and the co-editor of *Language in Her Eyes* and *The Expo Story*. She lives in Toronto.

Born in Winnipeg, DARREN WERSHLER-HENRY lives and works as a writer, editor and critic in Toronto. He is the author of two books of poetry, *NICHOLODEON: a book of lowerglyphs* and *the tapeworm foundry*, and the co-author of several books about the Internet.

EDMUND WHITE was born in Cincinnati in 1940. His fiction includes the autobiographical trilogy *A Boy's Own Story, The Beautiful Room Is Empty* and *The Farewell Symphony*, as well as *Caracole, Forgetting Elena, Nocturnes for the King of Naples* and his most recent work, *The Married Man*. He lives in New York City.

RUDY WIEBE is the author of several short story collections and eight novels, including *The Temptations of Big Bear* and *A Discovery of Strangers*. His most recent book is the award-winning non-fiction book *Stolen Life*, which tells the life story of his co-author Yvonne Johnson. He lives in Edmonton.

C. K. WILLIAMS's most recent books of poetry are *The Vigil*, published in 1997, and *Repair*, published in 1999, which won the Pulitzer Prize. His other works include a book of essays, *Poetry and Consciousness*, and a book of autobiographical meditation, *Misgivings*. A collection of his poems on love, *Love About Love*, is forthcoming. C. K. Williams teaches in the writing program at Princeton University.

MICHAEL WINTER is the author of *One Last Good Look*, a collection of stories, and *This All Happened*, a genre-defying work he calls a "journal-a-clef." Michael Winter lives and writes in Toronto and St. John's.

RONALD WRIGHT was born in England and lives in Ontario. His books include *Stolen Continents, Time Among the Maya* and, most recently, the dystopian novel *A Scientific Romance*, which was chosen a book of the year in three countries and won Britain's David Higham Prize for Fiction.